AS/A-Level Geography

KT-493-647

Investigative &
Research Skills
& Techniques

David Redfern

Malcolm Skinner

NORWICH CITY COLLEGE

Stock No.	238405	
Class	910.72	
Cat.		Proc	3WL

238   405

Philip Allan Updates, an imprint of Hodder Education, part of Hachette UK,
Market Place, Deddington, Oxfordshire OX15 0SE

Orders
Bookpoint Ltd, 130 Milton Park, Abingdon, Oxfordshire OX14 4SB
tel: 01235 827720
fax: 01235 400454
e-mail: uk.orders@bookpoint.co.uk
Lines are open 9.00 a.m.–5.00 p.m., Monday to Saturday, with a 24-hour
message answering service. You can also order through the Philip Allan
Updates website: www.philipallan.co.uk

© Philip Allan Updates 2008

ISBN 978-0-340-97243-4

First printed 2008
Impression number 5 4 3 2
Year 2013 2012 2011 2010 2009

All rights reserved; no part of this publication may be reproduced, stored in
a retrieval system, or transmitted, in any form or by any means, electronic,
mechanical, photocopying, recording or otherwise without either the prior
written permission of Philip Allan Updates or a licence permitting restricted
copying in the United Kingdom issued by the Copyright Licensing Agency
Ltd, Saffron House, 6–10 Kirby Street, London EC1N 8TS.

Printed in Spain.

Hachette UK's policy is to use papers that are natural, renewable and recyclable
products and made from wood grown in sustainable forests. The logging and
manufacturing processes are expected to conform to the environmental regula-
tions of the country of origin.

P01247

Contents

Introduction

Students have been required to undertake geographical research and investigative work, including fieldwork, at A-level for many years, but this does not mean that they find the organisation of such work easy. The new AS/A2 specifications in geography all state that fieldwork and the subsequent examination of investigative and enquiry skills are necessary for all students.

The assessment of this work takes one of two routes:
- ▶ a written examination paper, which seeks to test both fieldwork skills and other investigative research skills, often based on stimulus material
- ▶ a written examination paper, based on pre-release material, which seeks to test investigative skills based on both primary and secondary data

The purpose of this book is to guide you, the student, through both of these alternatives.

The first section deals with the nature and process of an investigation in general. It explains how to establish a suitable title, collect data, present and analyse material, and how to write up the final report if necessary. Most specifications expect a student to have completed the full process of an investigation prior to answering questions in an examination on that process.

The second section looks in more detail at the various types of assessment offered by the three examination boards in England. In this section, example questions from AQA, Edexcel and OCR are provided, together with guidance on how they can be answered and an explanation of how they will be assessed.

You may choose to read this book from cover to cover or, more likely, you will read the relevant section when you come to that point in your course. It is intended to act as a personal guide or tutor, enabling you to see where to go next and, ultimately, how to maximise your marks. We hope that this will keep you on the right track for success.

The geographical investigation

What is a geographical investigation?

All AS/A-level geography specifications require students to undertake investigative work, based on evidence from primary sources (including fieldwork) and secondary sources. In most cases a combination of both primary and secondary source material will be used.

In simple terms **primary data** are those collected by you in the field, or material from other sources that needs to be processed (e.g. census data, electoral rolls, remote-sensed data). **Secondary data** are derived from published documentary sources and have already been processed.

Primary research is essential — you must have had some direct contact with the area of study and/or the subject of investigation. This may involve a specific physical area, an identified group of people or a local issue. You must have visited the area, talked to the people or recorded other data there.

All geographical investigations should follow the same stages of enquiry:
▶ identification of the aim of the enquiry, often in the form of testing a hypothesis or establishing research questions
▶ collection of data, for example by measuring, mapping, observations, questionnaires, interviews or the use of ICT, e.g. geographical information systems, remote sensing
▶ organisation and presentation of the data using cartographic, graphic or tabular forms, with the possible use of ICT
▶ analysis and interpretation of the data, noting any limitations
▶ drawing together the findings of the investigation, evaluating them and formulating a conclusion
▶ awareness of the problems involved in undertaking geographical investigations/research
▶ suggested extensions to the investigation, including additional research questions that may have been stimulated by the findings
▶ a statement of success or otherwise of the investigation, with some commentary on the significance of the investigation for others

The geographical investigation therefore provides an opportunity for you to demonstrate what you can do beyond the examination room. Most investigative research of this type allows you to reflect on the connections between diverse elements of the subject — by definition, therefore, such work is synoptic.

It also allows you to build up evidence for the achievement of all the key skills, and enables you to submit a portfolio for the key skills qualification. Your investigation could demonstrate aspects of the following key skills:

▶ **Communication:**
  - read and synthesise information
  - write different types of documents
▶ **Application of number:**
  - plan and interpret information from different sources
  - carry out multi-stage calculations
  - present findings, explain results and justify choice of methods
▶ **Information technology:**
  - plan and use different sources to search for and select information
  - explore, develop and exchange information and derive new information
  - present information including text, numbers and images

Rarely should fieldwork be carried out alone. Hence, the key skill 'working with others' will be addressed, as will the other skills of 'improving own learning and performance' and 'problem solving', by the very nature of the task.

How do the examination boards assess investigative skills?

The examination boards assess investigative skills in different ways:
▶ a written examination paper, which seeks to test both fieldwork skills and other investigative research skills, often based on stimulus material
▶ a written examination paper, based on pre-release material, which seeks to test investigative skills based on both primary and secondary data

Some of the examination boards make use of more than one of these in their assessment programme, and it is essential that you check the requirements of your particular board. Table 1 provides a summary of the requirements of the three geography specifications in England.

Check your specification for the following:
▶ In which assessment units are investigative skills assessed?
▶ What are the restrictions on the titles or areas of study?

▶ Which specifications and assessment units offer an alternative?

▶ Which assessment units are based on pre-release material?

The proportion of the final marks carried by the investigative work varies from 15% to 20%, depending on the specification. Whatever the proportion, these marks are very much within your control. The purpose of this book is to guide you through the investigative process. Take advantage of this opportunity to boost your performance and maximise your overall grade.

Table 1 *Different requirements for the investigation and skills units for each of the major specifications*

	AQA	OCR	EDEXCEL
Which units and when?	AS Unit 2 (Geographical skills) A2 Unit 4A (Geography fieldwork investigation) A2 Unit 4B (Geographical issue evaluation)	A2 Unit F764 (Geographical skills)	AS Unit 2 (Geographical investigations) A2 Unit 4 (Geographical research)
Restrictions on topic	Unit 2 Question 1 (skills based) set in the context of one of the two core topics: Rivers, floods and management; or Population change. Question 2: fieldwork-related question based on the content of Unit 1 Unit 4A: question based on fieldwork which must be linked to the specification content Unit 4B: topic (from anywhere in the specification) issued 8 weeks in advance	Unit F764: a test of the skills of geographical research and investi-gations/fieldwork acquired during AS and A2, based on any of the topics studied at AS and A2 in Units F761, 762 and 763 Section A: one from three structured questions based on stimulus material and research skills Section B: two extended writing questions on research skills	Unit 2: two questions to be answered: one on a physical topic (Extreme weather or Crowded coasts), one on a human topic (Unequal spaces or Rebranding places). Candidates must use their own ideas from relevant fieldwork and research Unit 4: choice of one from six options. One long essay on the results of the research undertaken
Written Units	Unit 2: 1 hour Units 4A/4B: $1\frac{1}{2}$ hours	Unit F764: $1\frac{1}{2}$ hours	Unit 2: 1 hour Unit 4 : $1\frac{1}{2}$ hours
Pre-release material	Unit 4B: context of exercise (AIB) released 8 weeks in advance of examination	N/A	Unit 4: research focus material released 4 weeks in advance of examination

Establishing a suitable title for your investigation

Aims, hypotheses, research questions and objectives

The **aim** is a broad statement of what you are trying to achieve in your fieldwork. This will depend on the time available, the nature of the prevailing environmental conditions, the equipment you have and the risk assessment you have undertaken. For example, your aim might be:

▶ *To establish the social provision of services in a small residential area.*
▶ *To examine how a river changes downstream.*

Alternatively, you might want to express your aim as a question, called a **research question**:

▶ *Why does area G in town D appear to have more health-related services than area H?*
▶ *What factors influence channel characteristics on a small stretch of a local stream?*

You may also use questions to break down your overall aim into smaller subsections. Use two or three such questions, for example:

▶ *What management strategies have been used on the coastline at Y?*
▶ *How effective have the management strategies been at Y?*
▶ *What are the attitudes of people to the management strategies used at Y?*

A **hypothesis** is a statement based on a geographical question, for example:

▶ *A number of factors cause flooding to occur at P.*
▶ *A range of management strategies are used to protect area P from flooding.*
▶ *Not everyone thinks the flood management strategies at P are effective.*

In summary, for both research questions and hypotheses, the outcomes can be either measured or identified.

It is important to start collecting resources about both the specific area and the general theme you have chosen early in the process. Note that for each of the above, you should be aware of the concepts and ideas (sometimes referred to as the **underpinning theory**) that have led to the idea for the fieldwork in the first place. Make sure you have done research into these concepts and ideas before beginning the exercise.

Objectives are statements of how you will achieve your aim. What data will be needed to identify areas of decline/growth? How can these data be collected, analysed and presented? How will you obtain evidence of reasons/causes? Do you need to write to anyone, interview anyone or devise a questionnaire? What precise form of fieldwork needs to be undertaken?

Risk assessments are important too. Ensure that what you do is safe and that others know where you will be. Be fully aware of what you have done to be safe — you may face questions on this in the examination.

What is a null hypothesis?

Some investigations are best suited to the approach of establishing a **null hypothesis**. This takes the form of a negative assertion, which states that

there is *no* relationship between two chosen sets of variables. For example, a null hypothesis could state that *there is no relationship between air temperatures and distance from a city centre.* An alternative hypothesis can then be established, namely that *temperatures decrease with distance from a city centre.*

The null hypothesis assumes that there is a high probability that any observed relationships between the two sets of data (temperature and distance from a city centre) are due to unpredictable factors. If temperatures are seen to decrease with distance from the city centre, it is a result of chance. However, if the null hypothesis can be rejected statistically, we can infer that the alternative hypothesis can be accepted.

One benefit of this seemingly reverse approach to an enquiry is that if the null hypothesis cannot be rejected, it does not mean that a relationship does not exist — it may simply mean that not enough data have been collected to reject it. In short, the investigation was not worthless, but was too limited in scope. Another benefit of this approach is that it allows the use of statistical tests on the significance of the results to be carried out.

This is a sophisticated way in which to approach an enquiry and should only be used when fully understood.

Checking the feasibility of your investigation

Before embarking on this major piece of work that will, if successfully done, take a great deal of your time to complete, you should check whether or not the tasks involved are achievable and that an overall conclusion will be forthcoming.

Here are some questions you should ask yourself to see if your idea can really work.

Is my topic area within the requirements of the specification?
You need to check the specification yourself or ask your teacher, or you may have to have prior notification from the examination board.

Is the subject matter narrow enough?
In general, it is better to study one aspect in detail than several aspects sketchily, for example to study one river rather than three. Many investigations are best suited to a local area of study — one that is large enough to give meaningful results but not so large that it becomes unmanageable. Can you visit the area of study (you may have to do so on more than one occasion)? Again, seek guidance from your teacher on the scale of study for your chosen topic.

Will I be able to collect the data I need?
Remember, the use of primary data is paramount, and a whole range of sources of primary data exists — both quantitative and qualitative (see Table 2).

Table 2 *Primary data sources*

Quantitative	Qualitative
Land-use transects	Questionnaires
Housing surveys	Interviews
Environmental impact assessments	Field sketches
Photographs (taken by you)	
Traffic counts	
Climate surveys	
River measurements	
Soil surveys	

As the examination boards place great emphasis on data collection, it is wise to use a variety of data sources for your investigation. Do not use only questionnaires.

Will I be able to complete the investigation within the time period allowed?
An investigation that deals with changes over time (that is, one that involves a 'before' and an 'after' element) must be carefully monitored. Examples of such an investigation would include the impact of a new bypass around a settlement or the impact of a new retail park. Check that data for both time periods can be collected before you begin your investigation.

What equipment will I need?
The amount and nature of the equipment will obviously depend on the nature of the data to be collected. However, you do need to check that the equipment is available and in working order.

What else do I need to do?
Here is a final checklist of some of the main requirements of any fieldwork or data collection:
▶ **Always ask for permission if it is needed** – any investigation that involves you entering land or a building belonging to others will require permission from the owner. In most cases, a letter or telephone call explaining the purpose of your visit will suffice. It is often best to ask your teacher to write a short note on school- or college-headed paper in support of your work.
▶ **Check that you can get to your research area and back** – is there public transport to the area or will you need help? Note that fieldwork is often undertaken at weekends, and Sunday timetables are frequently different.
▶ **Wear appropriate clothing** – if you are going into remote and difficult areas, you must wear clothing that is warm and waterproof. Take special care with footwear, even in urban areas.
▶ **Be safety conscious** – *never* work alone and always tell someone where you are working. If possible, give expected time of return and methods of travel. Be particularly careful in coastal areas: check tide times and levels, never work underneath crumbling cliffs and stay on coastal paths.

Collecting primary data

Once you have established the aim and hypotheses of your investigation, you need to decide on the data required and what method of collection will be necessary. Investigations at AS/A-level are essentially based upon your own observations. This means collection of primary data through such techniques as questionnaires, interviews, river measurements, pedestrian surveys and urban transects. Your entire investigation can be based on such material but, depending on the scope of your work, it should be possible to include some secondary data from previously published sources.

Sampling

Sampling is used when it is impossible, or simply not necessary, to collect large amounts of data. Collecting small amounts of carefully selected data enables you to obtain a representative view of the feature as a whole. You cannot, for example, interview all the shoppers in a market town or all the inhabitants of a village but you can look at a fraction of those populations and, from that evidence, indicate how the whole is likely to behave.

Once you have established the need for a sample survey, you then have to decide upon a method that will ensure that a sufficiently large body of evidence is collected objectively. If, for example, you are interviewing the inhabitants of a village, who are of a variety of ages, you should not hold the bulk of your interviews with young members of the opposite sex as this will distort your picture of the settlement. There are a number of sampling techniques; the main ones to be considered here are random, systematic and stratified (quota).

Types of sampling

A **random sampling** is one that shows no bias and in which every member of the population has an equal chance of being selected. The method usually involves the use of random number tables.

In **systematic sampling** the sample is collected in a consistent manner by the selection, for example, of every tenth person or house. On a beach, you could decide to sample sites every 100 m along the feature; at each location you could use a quadrat (see below), selecting pebbles at the intersection points within the grid at regular intervals.

Stratified sampling is based on knowing something in advance about the population or area in question. For example, if you are surveying a population and you know its age distribution, your sample must reflect that age distribution. If you know the distribution of soil types in an area you are surveying, sites should be chosen in proportion to the area covered by each type of soil.

Bias in sampling

It is possible, through poor choice of method or insufficient evidence when sampling, to achieve a result that is unrepresentative of the population in question. Taking samples on the same day of the week or outside the same shop could lead to a distortion in a shopping survey, for example.

The size of the sample

The size of sample needed usually depends upon the complexity of the survey used. For a questionnaire, it is usually thought necessary to ask a sufficient number of people to take into account the considerable variety introduced by the range of questions used. Sample size can be restricted by practical difficulties, which can act as a limit to collection and the reliability of results. Your aim should be to keep the sampling error as small as possible. You are not a professional sampler and cannot be expected to conduct hundreds of interviews but, on the other hand, sampling only 20–30 people in a market survey would simply not be representative of the population as a whole.

Point sampling

Point sampling is carried out in surveys that involve, for example, studies of land use, vegetation cover, soil sites, and selection of such items as pebbles in longshore drift studies. Point sampling involves the use of a grid — that produced by Ordnance Survey is ideal, but for field surveys a quadrat can be used. A quadrat is a frame enclosing an area of known size (often 1 m²) and subdivided using wire or string. Both random and systematic sampling can be carried out within this framework.

Questionnaires

Many investigations at AS/A-level involve the use of questionnaires, the writing of which can be one of the most time-consuming and difficult aspects of an individual investigation.

Examiners often feel that questionnaires are badly designed, with an insufficient balance between specific questions and the more open-ended type. Open questions can certainly produce material that is less quantifiable, but they can also provide additional information that is vital in explaining behaviour revealed in answers to the more direct questions.

Questionnaire surveys in supermarket/hypermarket studies, for example, often involve a great deal of effort but reveal little more than very basic information on the behaviour of shoppers. Oddities in the pattern may not be accounted for because of a failure to include open questions that may have gone some way to revealing shoppers' motives for their behaviour.

Questionnaires can become far too sociological, and therefore of limited geographical value, by not concentrating on the spatial aspects of the sample being studied. Questionnaires that represent little more than a social survey should be avoided, as they will give little scope for mapping and analysis of pattern.

At GCSE, you were often asked to undertake a questionnaire survey in order to demonstrate your ability to complete it. At AS and A-level, the aim is completely different: quality, quantity and reliability of the data produced are as important as the means by which they were obtained.

When attempting a questionnaire survey there are a number of guidelines to follow:
- keep it as simple as possible — busy people do not like answering a lot of questions
- try to write a mix of closed (yes/no answers or multiple choice) and open questions (choice of answers or free statements)
- decide on a sample size that is adequate
- always try to introduce your questionnaire in the same way (write a brief introduction)
- put the questions in a logical sequence
- ask questions that will produce data that can be analysed
- think carefully about sensitive questions and use tick boxes for such information
- for respondents' ages and other personal information, it is often better to offer categories rather than insisting upon an exact figure
- try to ask questions about a person's behaviour, not about how he or she perceives his or her behaviour
- pilot your questionnaire to see if it will produce the material that you want
- always seek approval from your teacher or tutor before proceeding, to help you avoid insensitive questions and also to prevent harassment of local people by swamping the area with too many questionnaires
- obtain a document from your school/college that states exactly what you are doing
- always be polite, look smart and smile, and do not get upset if people refuse to answer
- *never* work alone
- if you intend to stand outside a specific service or in a shopping centre, it is a good idea to ask for permission

Interviews

It may be necessary for you to conduct interviews to ascertain people's opinions on an issue or to establish how they would act in certain circumstances. For example, in an investigation of rural land use, interviews with farmers may help to account for some of the changes that you have observed. If you are investigating a conflict, it is essential that you try to obtain the views of all the parties involved. This will take you beyond the scope of a questionnaire, as you will need to put different questions to each respondent or group involved. It is not always possible to meet the people concerned, so you may have to write to a person or group to ask for their opinions.

Interviews give you the opportunity to explore areas in more detail and to follow up any points that are raised. They can be time-consuming, so you are advised to think carefully before deciding upon such a course of action, and if you decide to proceed, use the technique sparingly.

Always send a well-written letter asking for the interview. Prepare for the interview well, as people do not like wasting their time. Being prepared means that you have a list of direct questions to ask, making sure that the person to whom you are speaking has the information you require.

Do not ask questions where you could obtain the information for yourself. Make notes at the interview or immediately afterwards. You could record the interview, but always obtain permission to do this before you start. Your final presentation can be very much enhanced by quotations from interviews, but always check accuracy and ask permission from the interviewee.

Sampling attitudes

Collecting information on people's attitudes is often difficult. You can ask about an individual's attitude during an interview, but if you are using a questionnaire survey you must phrase questions in such a way as to avoid bias creeping into your final results. There are three main ways of collecting such information:

▶ **Bi-polar tests** involve establishing a rating scale based upon two extremes of attitude (i.e. poles apart). For example, in a survey in the central business district (CBD), you could ask shoppers if they found the shopping area attractive or ugly and offer them a sliding scale of response, e.g. from (1) Ugly to (7) Attractive. You could put a number of such points to them and, as a result, give the area an overall rating. This would be useful when comparing shopping centres.

▶ A **point-score scale** is used to give respondents the chance to identify factors that they consider to be important. You could ask them to place the importance of each factor in attracting shoppers to a retailing centre on a scale from 0 to 4, for example.

▶ Using a **rating scale** allows respondents to agree or disagree with a statement. They could be asked to indicate their response to statements by choosing from categories ranging from 'Strongly agree' to 'Strongly disagree'.

Types of survey

So far we have shown you how to collect information by asking people questions. There are other types of survey that do not involve people and that you will find useful in obtaining information. Here are some of them, in many cases with details of how to proceed.

Surveys in urban areas

A large and varied number of surveys can be carried out within the context of urban fieldwork. Some of these are outlined below.

▶ **Land-use surveys** can be used for both rural and urban areas and must always be carried out with a clear purpose in mind. Land use should be placed into categories of similar uses. Sub-groups within categories should be established, depending upon the detail required. For example, several categories of housing can be recognised, such as terraced, detached, bungalows, semi-detached and flats.

▶ **Land-use transects** are used when the urban area is too large to survey as a whole, so a sample has to be taken. The transect is essentially a slice through the urban area to see how land use varies from one area to another. The transect will usually start in the middle of the urban area and run along a radial road to the urban fringe. Such surveys are often used to show how the land use on one side of an urban area differs from that on another. It can also be used to show where CBD functions cease and others take over, and therefore to delineate that central area. As well as land use, other information collected on a transect could include building height, number of storeys, upper-floor use, building condition (using an index of decay) and the age of buildings. It is also possible to collect information other than that concerned with urban geography in this way. Such projects could include noise and pollution surveys, and temperature/humidity readings across an urban area.

▶ **Environmental surveys** can be carried out as a form of appraisal or assessment, and the use of a point-score scale is recommended. In such cases, both positive and negative observations can be made. Environmental surveys can be used in urban areas, on beaches, and within river channels and valleys. This can be done by first-hand observations and by interviews with local residents or, in the case of recreation and tourist areas, with visitors. Noise, water and air pollution can also be studied. It is possible to use instruments and chemical testing kits in such surveys but there are simple tests that you can undertake using your own observations. Noise pollution can be estimated using a simple table, providing the same person makes all the observations. Air pollution can be assessed with the aid of a roll of sticky tape with which you can take samples from different surfaces in various parts of a town. Water pollution can be visually assessed (or by smell!), but it is possible to use a chemical kit or a secchi disc. This is a black and white disc that can be lowered into the water. The depth at which it is no longer visible and at which it comes into view again when lifted is recorded.

▶ **Shop location/shopping quality surveys** can be carried out in the CBD or even in the urban area as a whole. Shop location studies usually take place in the central area, with the aim of finding distinct patterns of land use within the CBD. Selected shop categories can then be analysed using the technique of nearest neighbour analysis, which indicates the degree to which the category is clustered. You could calculate an index of dispersion. (Such surveys could also be carried out on service outlets and offices within the urban area.) Shopping quality surveys can involve observational data or the use of a questionnaire.

▶ **Land value/house price surveys** are often used to identify the peak land value point (PLVP)/peak value intersection (PVI) in an urban area. Using property values from estate agents and newspapers is much easier than trying to find the value of property from local council tax assessments (which are open to inspection at the local authority's valuation office). Values should be converted into a unit per square metre of ground floor space.

▶ **Traffic flow surveys** can measure the traffic flow past several survey points within the urban area.

▶ **Pedestrian flow surveys** are a recognised means of indicating commercial activity within a CBD. There are a number of points to remember when contemplating such a survey:
  ● you will not be able to carry this out by yourself
  ● mornings and afternoons are best, so avoiding the movement of office workers that takes place in the middle of the day
  ● carry out more than one survey in order to contrast different times of day or even of the week
  ● at busy points, use two counters operating, if possible, back-to-back in the middle of the pedestrian throughway
  ● shopping centres are usually private property, so it is advisable to ask for permission

Surveys in physical geography
Within the realm of physical geography there are a number of surveys that can be carried out. Some of the more popular are outlined below.

▶ **River surveys** involve taking measurements that are then used to calculate fluvial features such as discharge, load, friction and efficiency. The most popular seems to be the calculation of the discharge of a river, which involves finding the cross-sectional area at certain points and multiplying it by the calculated speed (usually obtained from a flow meter) to give a figure expressed in cumecs (cubic metres per second). The calculation of the cross section also identifies the wetted perimeter. Other calculations or measurements that can be made include the gradient of the stream and the shape and size of the bed load. A final measurement to consider is the extent to which the river meanders — its index of sinuosity.

▶ **Surveys on slopes** usually involve calculating the steepness by means of a clinometer, measuring tape and ranging poles. One measurable feature of slopes is the amount and type of vegetation present, information that can be displayed on a kite diagram (see page 29).

▶ **Soil surveys** can be carried out on slopes, choosing sites in exactly the same way as you would for vegetation surveys. Various tests can be done, including: soil acidity (using a chemical soil-testing kit); soil texture (using a technique of feeling the texture with your fingers to find the sand, silt and clay elements); and moisture and organic content (by taking a sample, weighing it, drying it overnight and re-weighing, burning off the organic matter to leave the inorganic matter, the weight of which can be compared with that of the original sample).

▶ **Coastal surveys** could involve measuring the direction and amount of longshore drift and examining the structure of sand dunes, including the environment for plants and animals.

▶ **Glaciation surveys** in the field usually involve a study of glacial deposits, called till fabric analysis. This is based upon the idea that stones within the ice will become orientated in a direction that presents minimal resistance. This means that in glacial deposits they should be found with their long axis parallel to the direction of ice movement. From this you should be able to establish the direction of ice movement and possibly its source.

▶ **Microclimate surveys** can be carried out in your local area, possibly from rural to urban areas or across an urban area. Other contrasts could be made between day and night conditions or, more ambitiously, between seasons.

Field sketches and photographs

Both field sketches and photographs are excellent ways of recording observations you have made as part of your investigation. Field sketches enable you to pick out those features within the landscape that you consider important. Investigations in physical geography lend themselves nicely to this technique, particularly those on coastlines and glaciation. It does not matter if you cannot draw particularly well; it is far more important to produce a clear drawing with useful annotations.

If you are not a confident artist, try photography as an alternative. Remember, however, that far too many photographs find their way into the final presentation as attractive space fillers, in the mistaken belief that they will make it 'look good'. You need to select carefully the images that you want to show. As with sketches, annotation is vital: photographs are only useful if you point out to the reader the major features that you have observed. Photographs should be included at the relevant points in the text and not in a large block, which sometimes makes it very difficult for the reader to see their purpose.

Collecting secondary data

Secondary data collection involves gathering data that have already been put into written, statistical or mapped form. For an investigation at AS/A-level, there is a wide range of sources that can be accessed.

If your investigation has a temporal context, it is almost certain that you will need to access secondary data from previous surveys in the course of your work. Secondary material can be useful in the early stages of an investigation, where it can provide a helpful context. It can also be used when explaining and discussing primary material. You might also find it useful to combine field data with those obtained from newspapers, maps, census returns, local authority and other secondary sources. This should give you a much wider database for your analysis and for comparing material recorded first hand in the field with other results previously obtained.

When using secondary data, it is important to check the accuracy of the material, particularly if the information could be biased. Details of author, title, publication, date etc. must be incorporated within your final work; it is often a good idea to make reference to secondary material in your text by the use of footnotes or brackets.

Remember that when using secondary information there is a distinction between plagiarism and the acquisition of material by research. The distinction lies in the use you make of the information that you have obtained and the acknowledgement of sources used. If you include a direct quotation, you must use quotation marks, and you should also ensure that it is properly referenced.

Before you start an investigation, check that the sources you are intending to access have the information you need and that it is in a form you can use. It will make life very difficult if, at an advanced stage of your investigation, you find that your secondary sources do not match up with your primary research. A good example occurs in crime surveys. You may have carried out the primary research on an individual street basis, but when you come to access the secondary data, in this case urban crime figures, you will find that they are only available for each *district* within the urban area. It is therefore impossible to match them up with your more detailed data.

Sources of secondary material

▶ **National government material** is the source for a wide range of data, such as those concerned with the economy, employment, population and crime. Material is published by the Office for National Statistics and is available through Her Majesty's Stationery Office (HMSO), although this material can be expensive to buy and is best accessed through your local library or on the internet. The most helpful publications will probably be:
  - *Annual Abstract of Statistics*, which covers a wide range of data and has material for previous years
  - *Population Trends*
  - *Social Trends*
  - *Economic Trends*
  - *Monthly Digest of Statistics*, the best source of up-to-date information. You could also contact government agencies for information.

▶ **Other national sources** include:
  - the national media (newspapers, magazines and television/radio programmes)
  - charities
  - national organisations and action groups such as Shelter, English Heritage, The National Trust and The Countryside Commission
  - environmental pressure groups such as Greenpeace and Friends of the Earth
  - national company publications
  - the Meteorological Office

▶ **Local data** can be obtained from sources such as:
  - the local authority
  - the electoral register
  - your local library, which will have population statistics for areas as small as electoral wards (or Super Output Areas), census material going back to the nineteenth century and back copies of local newspapers, as well as photographic archives and photocopying facilities
  - the local Chamber of Commerce
  - estate agents
  - local newspapers
  - *Yellow Pages/Thomson Local Directory*
  - the local Health Authority (information on births, deaths, morbidity rates and mortality rates, and material relating to living conditions such as persons per room in households)
  - local action groups

▶ **Geographical material** comes from traditional sources, including:
  - geographical magazines and journals such as *Geography/Teaching Geography*, *Geographical Magazine*, *Geofile* and *Geography Review*

- maps and charts. Map sources include Ordnance Survey, Geological Survey, local authorities and Charles Goad, whose maps show the ownership of CBD property

▶ The **internet** offers an increasing number of sites that could be helpful in the course of a geographical investigation. However, do not waste time searching in the hope of finding something useful — have a definite purpose in mind before accessing this source. There is a great deal of information on government sites, particularly that of the Office for National Statistics (Neighbourhood Statistics). Some useful general sites are:

- **www.neighbourhood.statistics.gov.uk**
- **www.upmystreet.com**
- **www.ruralcommunities.gov.uk**
- **www.peopleandplanet.org**
- **www.un.org**
- **www.environment-agency.gov.uk**
- **www.metoffice.com**
- **www.oxfam.org.uk**
- **www.defra.gov.uk**
- **www.fao.org**
- **www.geographyfieldwork.com**

Presenting your results

Selecting the right technique

When you are ready to present your results, it is important that you use appropriate techniques. There is a wide range of techniques available to you — graphical, cartographic and tabular — but what you eventually select must be appropriate to the purpose of the investigation.

Such methods are rarely used as an end in themselves, but they are a significant element in analysis. They should be selected and applied to the data to enable you to describe any changes, establish any differences and identify relationships. Do not be tempted to use as many different techniques as possible as this can lead to similar data being presented in several different ways for no reason other than to show that you know how to construct various forms of maps and diagrams.

At AS/A-level, mark schemes award credit to those candidates who use or have used a suitable range of techniques that can provide the potential for analysis. Most investigations will include a choice of techniques along the following lines:

▶ identification or description of differences
▶ description of spatial patterns
▶ identification of relationships
▶ classification of data according to characteristics

Regardless of which technique you eventually choose as being the most appropriate to the circumstances, make sure that it is clear and easy to understand, that it is as simple as possible and that it helps you to convey the message to the person reading your report.

Main methods of presentation

Table 3 Methods of presenting data

Use	Graphical	Cartographic
Identifying differences	Line graphs (arithmetic and logarithmic) Cumulative frequency curves (including Lorenz curves) Pie/bar graphs Proportional symbols Histograms Long/cross sections Kite diagrams Radial diagrams	Pie graphs, bar graphs and proportional symbols can be placed on a base map to show spatial variations
Describing spatial patterns		Isopleths Choropleths Flow diagrams and desire lines
Identification of relationships	Scattergraphs	
Classification of data	Triangular graphs	

Arithmetic graphs

Arithmetic graphs are appropriate when you want to show *absolute changes* in the data (Figure 1). You will already be familiar with the use of such graphs, but there are a number of points you should be aware of if you intend to use this method at this level:

▶ It is usual to plot the independent variable on the horizontal axis and the dependent variable on the vertical. With temporal graphs, time should always be considered the independent variable and plotted horizontally.
▶ Try to avoid awkward scales and remember that the scale you choose should enable you to plot the full range of data for each variable.
▶ Axes should always be clearly labelled.
▶ If you are plotting more than one line, it is a good idea to use different symbols for the plots.
▶ You can put two sets of data on the same graph, using the two vertical axes to show different scales.

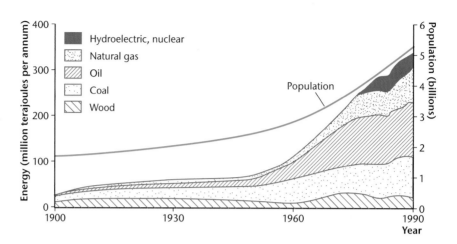

Figure 1
A compound line graph showing twentieth-century trends in world use of selected energy sources. Total world population is shown as a simple line

Logarithmic graphs

A logarithmic graph (Figure 2) is drawn as an *arithmetic line* graph except that the scales are divided into a number of cycles, each representing a ten-fold increase in the range of values. If the first cycle ranges from 1 to 10, the second will extend from 10 to 100, the third from 100 to 1,000 and so on. The scale can be started at any exponent of 10, from as low as 0.0001 up to 1 million; the starting point depends upon the range of data to be plotted.

Graph paper can be either fully logarithmic or semi-logarithmic (where one axis consists of one or more log cycles and the other is linear or arithmetic). Semi-logarithmic graphs are useful for plotting rates of change through time. If the rate of change is increasing at a constant, proportional rate (e.g. doubling each time period), it will appear as a straight line. In this case, you must plot time on the linear scale.

Logarithmic graphs are good for showing rates of change — the steeper the line, the faster the rate. They also allow a wider range of data to be displayed.

Remember that you cannot plot positive and negative values on the same logarithmic graph and that the base line of the graph is never zero, as this is impossible to plot on such a scale.

Logarithmic and semi-logarithmic graph paper for you to photocopy is provided on pages 52 and 53.

Lorenz curves

Lorenz curves are a form of cumulative frequency curve. They can be drawn on both arithmetic and logarithmic axes. Data are converted into percentages. The largest percentage is plotted first, and each consecutive number added on

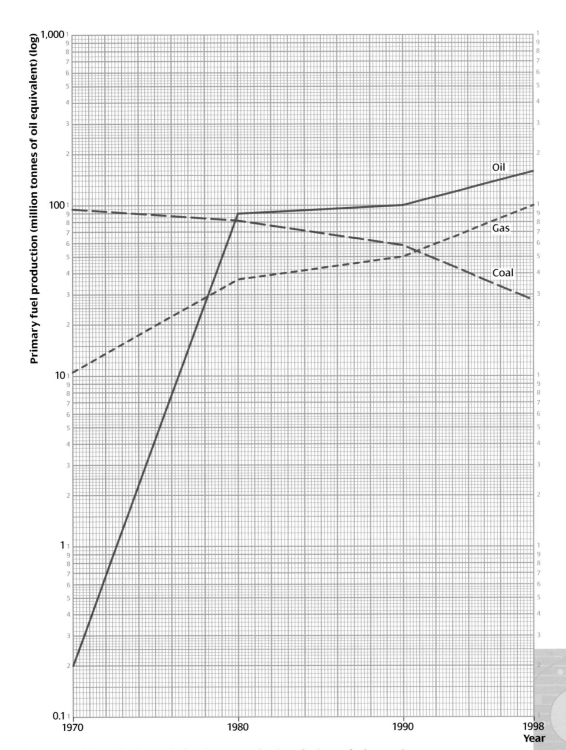

Figure 2 Semi-logarithmic graph showing UK production of primary fuels over time

cumulatively and plotted, until 100% is reached. For example, if the highest number is 50%, it is plotted at that point. If the second highest is 20%, then that is plotted at 70% (50 + 20), and so on until 100% is reached (Figure 3).

A Lorenz curve can be used to measure or illustrate the extent to which a geographical distribution is even or concentrated. In this case, the categories are ranked in order of size, with the largest first. The percentage value of the highest category is plotted first. The highest and second highest categories are then added together to give the next figure to plot. This continues until all the categories have been plotted and 100% has been reached. This could be used, for example, to plot the distribution of employment in an industry in relation to the workforce nationally (e.g. the distribution of all medical employment in a country against the distribution of all service employment in that country).

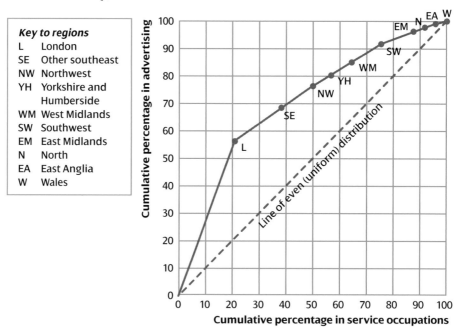

Figure 3 A Lorenz curve to show the cumulative percentage of service workers in advertising in the standard regions of the UK in relation to the cumulative percentage of employment in all service occupations

The location quotient, which is dealt with in the section on analysis below, is a method that represents such concentrations as a numerical value.

If it is not necessary to compare a distribution with a national or regional one, the cumulative percentage for your data set can simply be plotted in rank order. The vertical axis is labelled *cumulative percentage* (scale 1–100%) and the horizontal axis is labelled *rank order* (scaled to cover the total number of items in the set, e.g. eight categories will produce eight rank orders). This can allow comparisons with other distributions, and a line of perfect regularity can be drawn where there is the same percentage in each category. This method is often used for showing the division of employment between particular occupations or the dependence of a country upon certain types of energy (Figure 4).

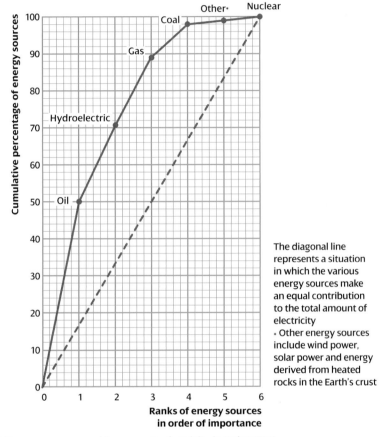

The diagonal line represents a situation in which the various energy sources make an equal contribution to the total amount of electricity

• Other energy sources include wind power, solar power and energy derived from heated rocks in the Earth's crust

Figure 4 Energy sources used to generate electricity in Italy (1995)

Pie graphs (or pie charts/divided circles) and bar graphs

The pie graph is divided into segments according to the share of the total value represented by each segment. This is a useful method as it is visually effective: the reader is able to see the relative contribution of each segment to the whole (Figure 5). On the other hand, it is difficult to assess percentages or make comparisons between individual pie charts if there are a lot of small segments.

The bar graph (or chart) has vertical columns rising from a horizontal base, the height of the column being proportional to the value it represents. The vertical scale can be used to represent absolute data or those data expressed in percentages.

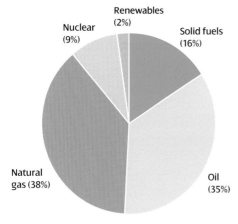

Figure 5 *Pie chart showing primary energy supply in the UK (2004)*

Bar graphs are easily understood and show relative magnitudes effectively (Figure 6). It is also possible to show positive and negative values if a scale is drawn through zero. For example, profit and loss can be shown on the same graph (a divergent graph, Figure 7).

Bar graphs are easy to read as the height of the bar can be read off the vertical scale. This makes them more useful than pie graphs in most cases. Students often produce bar graphs that are too complicated (for example, constructing too many multiple bars or using two different scales on the vertical axes). This loses the greatest assets of the method — simplicity and clarity of presentation.

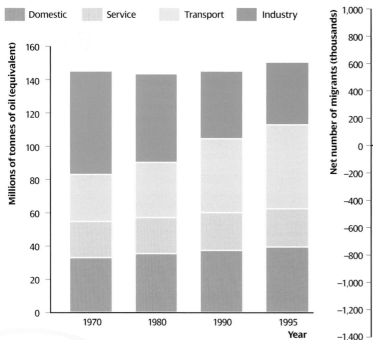

Figure 6 *A compound bar graph showing UK final energy consumption by sector, 1970–95*

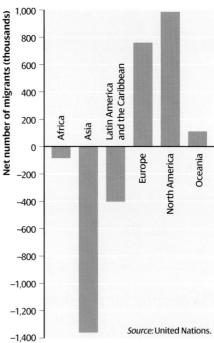

Figure 7 *A gain–loss bar chart showing annual net migration totals in the world's major areas (1990–95)*

Proportional symbols

Symbols can be used which are drawn proportional in area or volume to the value they represent.

We have already seen that the essential element in the construction of a bar graph is that the length of the column is proportional to the value it represents. This can be extended to pie graphs, where the circles can be drawn proportional to the total value.

Other symbols that can be used include squares, cubes and spheres. They can be drawn independently or placed on a map to show spatial differences (Figure 8). If you are using them in this way, it is important that the symbols are placed carefully on the map. It is essential to avoid too much overlap, but each symbol must 'have a sense of place' in that it must be clear which area the symbol is representing. In AS/A-level investigations, the most commonly used methods are the bar and the circle, as these are the easiest to construct.

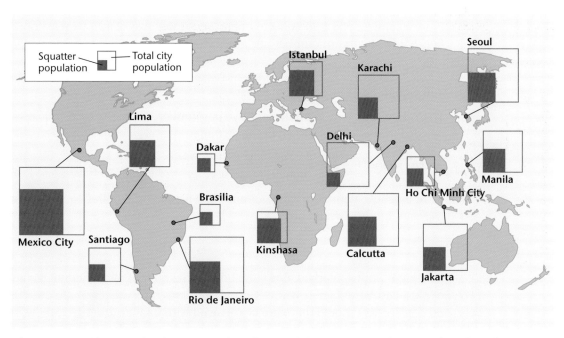

Figure 8 *Map with proportional squares to show the size of the squatter population in selected world cities (2000)*

Histograms

Histograms are used to show the frequency distribution of data. Bars are drawn to indicate the frequency of each class of data, but this method must not be confused with the bar graph/chart. Histograms are used to simplify and clarify data that are easier to analyse when placed into groups or classes, rather than being presented as individual figures. Large amounts of data can be reduced to more manageable proportions, which will allow you to see some of the trends present.

Before you can draw a histogram, you need to group the data and this can be difficult. The important principle is that you must illustrate differences between classes while keeping the variation within each class to an absolute minimum. You will need to establish:

▶ the number of classes to be used
▶ the range of values in each class, i.e. the class interval

The number of classes you use must depend upon the amount of data you have collected. Choose too many classes and you will have insufficient variation between them and may finish up with too many 'empty' classes; choose too few and you will have difficulty in recognising trends within the data. One method is to use the formula:

> number of classes = 5 × log of the total number of items in the set

If, for example, you had collected data about the size of 120 pebbles on a beach, the maximum number of classes would be:

$$5 \times \log 120 = 5 \times 2.08 = 10.4$$

You would therefore select ten classes.

The range of values is influenced by the number of classes that you have decided to use. This is shown in the formula:

$$\text{class interval} = \frac{\text{range of values (highest to lowest)}}{\text{number of classes}}$$

If, for example, your data ranged from 96 to 5 and you required four classes, the class interval would be:

$$\frac{96 - 5}{4} = 22.75$$

It is important to clearly define class boundaries so that all individual pieces of data can be assigned without problem. Class intervals of 0–25, 25–50, 50–75, 75–100 should therefore be replaced with 0–24.9, 25–49.9, 50–74.9, 75–100, which are now continuous classes with no overlap.

The decision on the number of classes and the class interval will be influenced by the type of data you are dealing with and the purpose to which they are being put. You will need to decide exactly what it is that you are trying to illustrate or analyse.

The resulting distribution will fit into one of three categories (Figure 9):
▶ If your distribution has a modal class in the middle with progressively smaller bars to both sides, it is similar to the **normal** distribution.
▶ If the modal class lies in the lower classes, the distribution is said to show **positive skew**.
▶ If it lies to the upper end, the distribution is said to show **negative skew**.

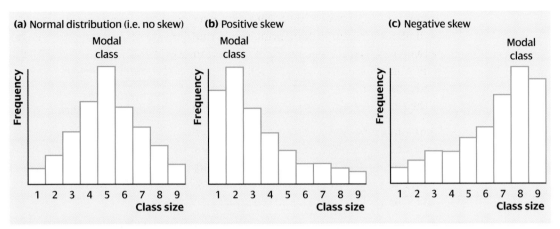

Figure 9 Histograms showing different distributions

Triangular graphs

Triangular graphs are plotted on special paper which is in the form of an equilateral triangle. Although at first this looks to be a method that has widespread application, it is only possible to use it for a whole number that can be broken down into three components expressed as percentages. Therefore, the triangular graph cannot be used for absolute data or for any figures that cannot be broken down into three components (Figure 10).

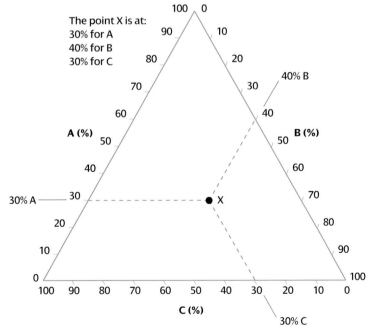

Figure 10 A triangular graph

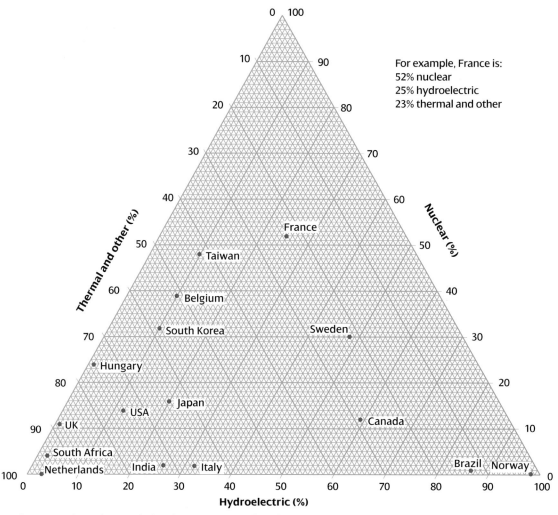

Figure 11 *Triangular graph showing percentage of total electricity production by generating source for selected countries (1988)*

The advantage of using this type of graph is that the varying proportions can be seen, indicating the relative importance of each. It is also possible to see the dominant variable of the three. After plotting, clusters will sometimes emerge, enabling a classification of the items involved (Figure 11). Triangular graph paper for you to photocopy is provided on page 54.

Scattergraphs

A scattergraph is used to investigate the relationship between two sets of data (Figure 12). In this book a scattergraph is included as a form of presentation, but it is equally useful for identifying patterns and trends that might lead to

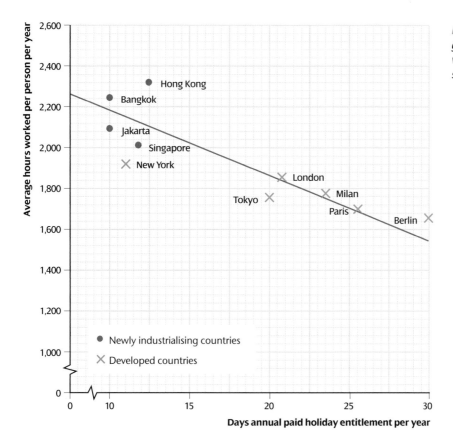

Figure 12 A scatter-graph showing working patterns in selected cities (2000)

further enquiry. If you use this method, there are several points to bear in mind:

▶ Scattergraphs can be plotted on arithmetic, logarithmic or semi-logarithmic graph paper.

▶ Use them only when you feel that there is a relationship to be investigated. It is possible for a correlation to emerge even when a relationship is just coincidental.

▶ One variable usually has an effect on the other and this enables you to identify the independent and dependent variables.

▶ The two variables are placed on the graph so that the independent variable is on the horizontal axis and the dependent variable on the vertical axis.

▶ A trend line can then be inserted by eye (a best fit line). If this runs from bottom left to top right, it indicates a positive relationship. If it runs top left to bottom right, it indicates a negative relationship.

▶ The closer the points are to the trend line, the stronger the relationship, but this should be assessed with a statistical test (see the Spearman rank correlation coefficient, page 37).

▶ Points lying some distance from the trend line are classed as residuals (anomalies). These can be referred to as either negative or positive. Identification of residuals can enable you to make further investigations into other factors that could influence your two selected variables.

There is a more accurate method to locate the trend line. This involves the use of 'semi-averages' to generate a regression line that summarises the characteristics of the scattergraph. The procedure is as follows:

▶ Calculate the mean value for the data on the independent axis (x) and the mean value for the data on the dependent axis (y).

▶ Use these two values as coordinates to plot a point on the scattergraph (A).

▶ Using only the values of x and y that are higher than the mean, calculate the upper semi-averages for these values and plot them as a point on the scattergraph (B).

▶ Repeat this process for those values that are lower than the mean to calculate the lower semi-averages, and again plot them as a point (C).

▶ Draw a regression line on the graph guided by the position of A, B and C. These three points may not form a perfect straight line but they can be used to obtain a more accurate placement for the trend line.

Long sections and cross sections

These methods are useful for describing and comparing the shape of the land. A graph showing height on the vertical scale against a horizontal scale of distance is constructed. Long sections are used mostly for river studies, while cross sections can be drawn for a number of landscape features.

The horizontal scale of your section is usually the same as that of the map with which you are working, but it is unusual to use the same vertical scale as the map. If you are working with a standard OS map, in most cases the scale would reduce your section to a line that would show little variation. It is therefore necessary to adopt a larger scale on the vertical axis, being careful not to exaggerate it massively and make the gentlest of slopes appear like the north face of the Eiger! This degree of exaggeration can be calculated and presented with your finished work. The same principles apply to both long- and cross-section construction.

Kite diagrams

Kite diagrams are a useful means of showing changes over distance, particularly in vegetation (Figure 13). One axis is used for distance and the other for individual plant species. The width of the kite, representing a single species, enables a visual comparison to be made of the distribution of vegetation at any point in the section.

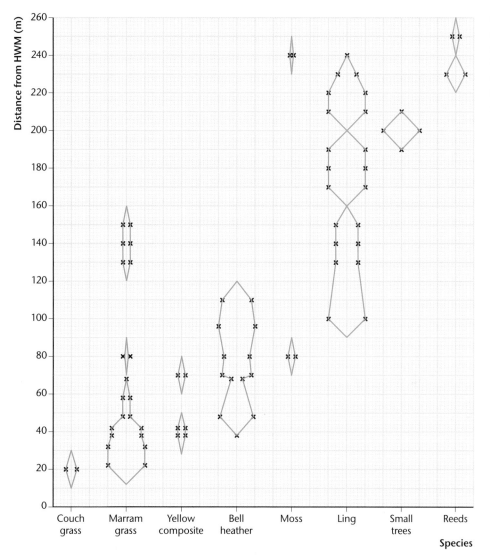

Figure 13
Kite diagram showing a transect across a dune area in Dorset

Radial diagrams

These graphs are particularly useful when one variable is a directional feature, for example wind rose diagrams show both the direction and the frequency of winds. The circumference represents the compass directions, and the radius can be scaled to show the percentage of time that winds blow from each direction.

Radial diagrams can also be used when one variable is a recurrent feature, such as a time period of 24 hours or an annual cycle of activity. They can be used to plot traffic flows or pedestrian flows over a period of time during the day, or monthly output figures (Figure 14).

Figure 14
Radial diagram showing pedestrian flow patterns in the CBD

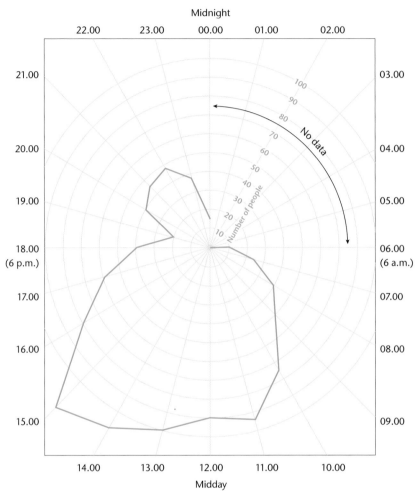

Such graphs should be used only for specific types of data. The scale around the circumference can only be used for a variable that is continuous, such as a repeating time sequence or the points of a compass.

Isopleth/isoline maps

When you collect data from different places, they can be represented as points on a map. It is possible to join all points of the same value on the map by a line. Such a map allows a pattern to be seen in a distribution. The best known example of such isolines (or isopleths) is on OS maps where the lines (contours) join places of the same height. This technique can be applied to a number of physical factors, such as rainfall (isohyets), temperature (isotherms) and pressure (isobars), as well as human factors, such as pedestrian densities in a CBD survey (Figure 15) or travel times (isochrones) for commuters and shoppers.

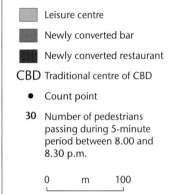

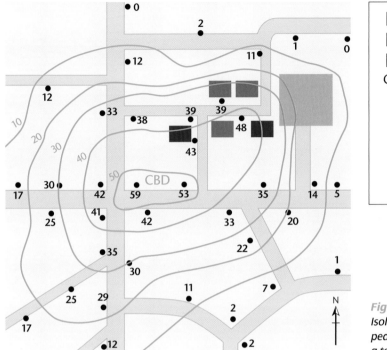

Figure 15
Isoline map showing pedestrian densities in a town centre

Choropleth maps

A choropleth is a map on which data values are represented by the density of shading of each area. The data are usually in a form that can be expressed in terms of area, such as population density per square kilometre.

To produce such a map certain stages must be followed:
▶ The material must be grouped into classes. Before you can do this you need to decide the number and range of classes required to display your data.
▶ You must devise a range of shadings to cover the range of your data. Darkest shades should represent the highest figures and vice versa. It is good practice not to use the two extremes of black and white; black suggests a maximum level, while white indicates that there is nothing within the area. A suitable method of shading is shown in Figure 16.

Choropleth maps are fairly easy to construct and are visually effective as they give the reader a chance to see general patterns in a real distribution. There are, however, a few limitations to the method:
▶ It assumes that the whole area under one form of shading has the same density, with no variations. For example, on maps of the UK the whole of Scotland may be covered by one category, when it is obvious that there could be large variations between the central populated areas and the Highlands.

Figure 16
A choropleth map showing population density in a metropolitan borough in northern England (2001)

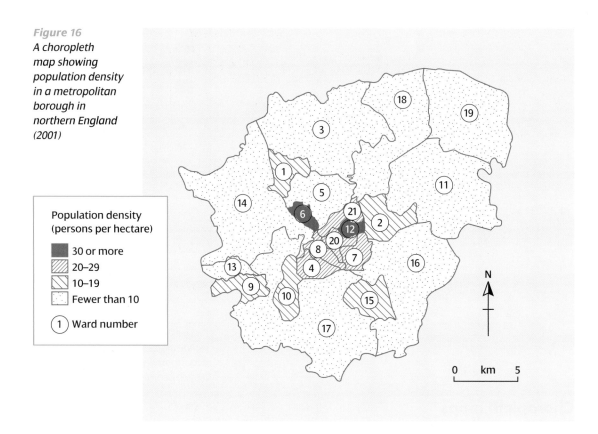

Population density (persons per hectare)

- ■ 30 or more
- ▨ 20–29
- ◪ 10–19
- ▫ Fewer than 10

① Ward number

▶ The method indicates abrupt changes at the drawn boundaries that will not be present in reality.

Flow lines, desire lines and trip lines

These three forms of presentation are similar in that they all represent the volume and direction of movement from place to place. They are useful to show such features as:

▶ traffic movements along particular routes (e.g. roads, railways and waterways)
▶ migrations of populations
▶ movement of goods or commodities between different regions
▶ movement of shoppers

For both flow lines and desire lines, the width of the line is proportional to the volume of movement. A flow line represents the quantity of movement along an actual route, such as a train or bus route (Figure 17). A desire line is drawn directly from the point of origin to the destination and takes no account of a specific route. Trip lines can be drawn, for example, to show where people shop, with lines linking a town to nearby villages (Figure 18).

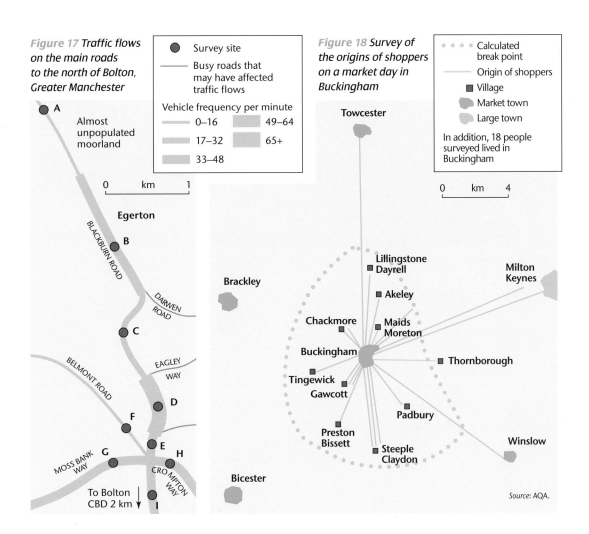

Figure 17 *Traffic flows on the main roads to the north of Bolton, Greater Manchester*

Survey site

Busy roads that may have affected traffic flows

Vehicle frequency per minute

0–16
17–32
33–48
49–64
65+

A

Almost unpopulated moorland

0   km   1

Egerton

BLACKBURN ROAD

B

DARWEN ROAD

C

BELMONT ROAD

EAGLEY WAY

D

F

E   H

G

MOSS BANK WAY

CROMPTON WAY

To Bolton CBD 2 km

I

Figure 18 *Survey of the origins of shoppers on a market day in Buckingham*

Calculated break point

Origin of shoppers

Village

Market town

Large town

In addition, 18 people surveyed lived in Buckingham

0   km   4

Towcester

Lillingstone Dayrell

Milton Keynes

Akeley

Brackley

Chackmore

Maids Moreton

Thornborough

Buckingham

Tingewick

Gawcott

Padbury

Preston Bissett

Winslow

Steeple Claydon

Bicester

Source: AQA.

The analysis and interpretation of data

The use of statistical analysis is a common feature of geographical investigations. Objective analysis of data can be used to support the conclusions suggested by a subjective view of the results of the investigation.

Statistical analysis should not be used just for show. It should assist in the evaluation of the significance of the results and form an integral part of the write-up of the investigation. There should be careful consideration of the most effective form of statistical analysis, and why that technique is appropriate.

It should be obvious that any statistical technique must be used correctly and all calculations performed accurately. It is perhaps less obvious that the result of any calculation should be supported by statements that explain what the mathematical result means. Many calculator and computer functions will complete the mathematical process for you, so it is essential that you understand the relevance of the values produced. In short, never use a statistical technique that you do not understand or in which you are not confident.

Table 4 summarises some of the major statistical techniques that are either required or suggested by the AS/A-level specifications of the major examination boards for use in either investigations or written examinations.

Table 4 **Statistical techniques**

Reason for using statistics	Statistical technique(s)
The summarising and comparison of data	Measures of central tendency: mean, mode, median
The dispersion and variability of data	Range Inter-quartile range (dispersion graphs) Standard deviation
The correlation of two sets of data	Spearman rank correlation coefficient and tests of significance
The degree of concentration of geographical phenomena	Location quotients
The measurement of patterns in a distribution	Nearest neighbour statistic
The degree to which there are differences between observed data and expected data, and the statistical significance of them	Chi-squared test Mann-Whitney U test

The following sections set out the means by which each of these techniques can be used and the rationale for their use.

Measures of central tendency

There are three measures: the arithmetic mean, the mode and the median.

Arithmetic mean ($\bar{x}$)
This is calculated by adding all values in a data set and dividing the total by the number of values in the set. So

$$\bar{x} = \frac{\Sigma x}{n}$$

The arithmetic mean is of little value on its own and should be supported by reference to the standard deviation of the data set.

Mode
This is the most frequently occurring value in a data set and can only be identified if all the individual values are known.

Median

This is the middle value in a data set when it is arranged in order of highest to lowest (that is, in rank order). There should be an equal number of values both above and below the median value. If the number of values in a data set is odd, the median will be the

$$\frac{(n+1)}{2}$$ item in the data set.

So, for example, if the total number of items in a data set is 27, the median will be the 14th value in the rank order of the data.

If the number of values in the data set is even, the median value is the mean of the middle two values. Any calculation of the median is best supported by a statement of the interquartile range of the data (see below).

Distribution of the data set

It is possible that each of these measures could give the same result, but they are more likely to give different results. The characteristics of the distribution of a data set would have to be perfectly 'normal' for the same result to be achieved with each measure, and this is extremely unlikely when using real data. It is more likely that the distribution of the data set is skewed. The more it is skewed, the greater the variation in the three measures of central tendency.

None of these measures gives a reliable picture of the distribution of the data set. It is possible for two different sets of data to give the same values for mean, mode and median. Consequently, measures of the dispersion or variability of the data should also be provided.

Measures of dispersion or variability

There are three measures of dispersion or variability: range, interquartile range and standard deviation.

Range

This is the difference between the highest value and the lowest value in a data set. It gives a simple indication of the spread of the data.

Interquartile range

The interquartile range is calculated by ranking the data in order of size and dividing them into four equal groups of quartiles. The boundary between the first and second quartile is known as the upper quartile, and the boundary between the third and fourth quartiles is the lower quartile. They can be calculated as follows:

▶ The upper quartile (UQ) is the $\frac{(n+1)}{4}$th item in the data set when arranged in rank order (from highest to lowest).

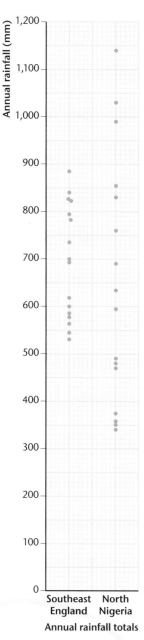

Figure 19
Dispersion graph showing rainfall in two selected locations over a 16-year period

▶ The lower quartile (LQ) is the $\frac{3(n+1)}{4}$ th item in the data set when arranged in rank order.

So the interquartile range (IQR) = UQ − LQ.

The IQR indicates the spread of the middle 50% of the data set about the *median* value, and thus gives a better indication of the degree to which the data are spread, or dispersed, on either side of the middle value.

Dispersion graphs

Dispersion graphs (Figure 19) are used to display the main patterns in the distribution of data. The graph shows each value plotted as an individual point against a vertical scale. It shows the range of the data and the distribution of each piece of data within that range. It therefore enables comparison of the degree of bunching of two sets of data.

Standard deviation

This measures the degree of dispersion about the *mean* value of a data set. It is calculated as follows:
▶ the difference between each value in the data set and the mean value are calculated
▶ each difference is squared, to eliminate negative values
▶ these squared differences are totalled
▶ this total is divided by the number of values in the data set, to provide the variance of the data
▶ the square root of the variance is calculated

$$\text{standard deviation} = \sqrt{\frac{\Sigma(\bar{x}-x)^2}{n}}$$

The standard deviation is statistically important as it links the data set to the normal distribution. In a normal distribution:
▶ 68% of the values in the data set lie within ± 1 standard deviation of the mean
▶ 95% of the values in a data set lie within ± 2 standard deviations of the mean
▶ 99% of the values in a data set lie within ± 3 standard deviations of the mean

A low standard deviation indicates that the data are clustered around the mean value and that dispersion is narrow. A high standard deviation indicates that the data are more widely spread and that dispersion is large. The standard deviation also allows comparison of the distribution of the values in a data set with a theoretical norm and is therefore of greater use than just the measures of central tendency.

Measuring correlation: the Spearman rank correlation coefficient

Comparisons are made between two sets of data in order to see if there is a relationship between them. However, even if there is a relationship, it does not prove a causal link. In other words, a relationship does not prove that a change in one variable has been responsible for a change in the other. For example, there may be a direct relationship between altitude and the amount of precipitation in a country such as the UK. These two variables (altitude and precipitation) are clearly linked, but a decrease in one does not automatically cause a decrease in the other — they are simply related to each other. There are two main ways in which comparisons can be shown:
▶ using scattergraphs (see page 26)
▶ measuring correlation using the Spearman rank correlation coefficient

The Spearman rank correlation coefficient is used to measure how much correlation there is between two sets of data (or variables). It gives a numerical value that summarises the degree of correlation, and therefore it is an example of an objective indicator. Once calculated, the numerical value has to be tested statistically to see how significant the result is.

The Spearman rank test can be used with any sets of data consisting of raw figures, percentages or indices that can be ranked. The formula for the calculation of the correlation coefficient is:

$$R_S = 1 - \frac{6\Sigma d^2}{n^3 - n}$$

where d is the difference in ranking of the two sets of paired data and n is the number of sets of paired data.

The calculation method is as follows:
▶ rank one set of data from highest to lowest (highest value ranked 1, second highest 2 and so on)
▶ rank the other set of data in the same way
▶ beware of tied ranks. To allocate a rank order to such values, calculate the average rank that they occupy. For example, if there are three values that should all be placed at rank 5, then add together ranks 5, 6 and 7 and divide by 3, giving an average rank of 6 for each one. The next value in the sequence would then be allocated rank 8
▶ calculate the difference in rank (d) for each pair of data in the two sets
▶ square each difference

▶ add the squared differences together and multiply by 6 (A)
▶ calculate the value of $n^3 - n$ (B)
▶ divide A by B and take the result away from 1

The answer should be a value between +1.0 (perfect positive correlation) and −1.0 (perfect negative correlation).

Some words of warning

▶ You should have at least ten sets of paired data, as the test is unreliable if n is less than 10.
▶ You should not use too many sets of paired data (maximum 30), or the calculations become complex and prone to error.
▶ Too many tied ranks can interfere with the statistical validity of the exercise, although it is appreciated that there is little you can do about real data.
▶ Be careful about choosing the variables to compare — do not choose dubious or spurious sets of data.

How to interpret the result

In trying to interpret the result of the Spearman rank test the following should be considered.

What is the direction of the relationship? If the calculation produces a positive value, the relationship is positive, or direct. In other words, as one variable increases, so does the other. If the calculation produces a negative value, the relationship is negative, or inverse.

How statistically significant is the result? When comparing two sets of data, there is always a possibility that the relationship demonstrated between them has occurred by chance. The figures in the data sets may just happen to have been the right ones to bring about a correlation. It is necessary, therefore, to assess the statistical significance of the result. In the case of the Spearman rank test, the critical values for R_s must be consulted. These can be obtained from statistical tables, but Table 5 below shows some examples of them.

According to statisticians, if there is a > 5% possibility of the relationship occurring by chance, the relationship is not significant. This is called the **rejection level**. The relationship could have occurred by chance more than five times in 100, and this is an unacceptable level of chance. If there is a < 5% possibility, the relationship is significant and therefore meaningful. If there is a < 1% possibility of the relationship occurring by chance, the relationship is very significant. In this case, the result could only have occurred by chance one in 100 times, which is very unlikely.

So how does this work? Having calculated a correlation coefficient, examine the critical values given in Table 5 (ignore the positive or negative sign).

Table 5 Critical values for R_s

n	0.05 (5%) significance level	0.01 (1%) significance level
10	± 0.564	± 0.746
12	0.506	0.712
14	0.456	0.645
16	0.425	0.601
18	0.399	0.564
20	0.377	0.534
22	0.359	0.508
24	0.343	0.485
26	0.329	0.465
28	0.317	0.448
30	0.306	0.432

If your coefficient is greater than these values, the coefficient is significant at that level. If your coefficient is smaller, the relationship is not significant at that level.

As an illustration, suppose you had calculated an R_s value of 0.50 from 18 sets of paired data. 0.50 is greater than the critical value at the 0.05 (5%) level, but not that at the 0.01 (1%) level. In this case, therefore, the relationship is significant at the 0.05 (5%) level, but not at the 0.01 (1%) level.

Worked example: Spearman rank test
Survey: size of shingle along a storm beach

The beach in question is aligned from southwest to northeast and the dominant approach of the waves is from the southwest. The main ridge appears to increase in height with distance from the southwest. The shingle appears to decrease in size and become more rounded towards the northeast. This may indicate that the direction of longshore drift is from the southwest to the northeast, meaning that the further the shingle is moved, the more it is affected by attrition and, therefore, reduced in size. A scattergraph would show the general trend of the relationship between distance and size. However, there are anomalies, so a correlation test would be useful to decide the strength of that relationship. The raw data are shown in Table 6.

The data required for the calculation of R_s between distance and the mean shingle size are shown in Table 7.

$$R_s = 1 - \frac{6\Sigma d^2}{n^3 - n}$$

$$\Sigma d^2 = 996.5$$

$$R_s = 1 - \frac{6 \times 996.5}{15^3 - 15}$$

Table 6 *The characteristics of shingle along a storm beach*

Distance from SW end of beach (m)	Height (m)	Mean shingle diameter (cm)	Roundness index
60	5.5	8.4	1.72
180	7.5	8.5	1.77
300	8.0	7.7	1.63
420	11.5	8.1	1.48
540	11.0	6.1	1.58
660	7.5	5.8	1.63
780	10.0	6.2	1.60
900	10.5	7.2	1.41
1,020	10.0	7.5	1.36
1,120	11.0	6.2	1.33
1,220	14.0	6.5	1.35
1,340	12.5	5.8	1.23
1,460	18.0	4.8	1.18
1,580	13.5	5.0	1.17
1,700	15.0	5.8	1.25

Table 7 *Data for the calculation of R_s*

Distance (m)	Rank	Mean shingle diameter (cm)	Rank	Difference in rank (d)	d^2
60	15	8.4	2	13	169
180	14	8.5	1	13	169
300	13	7.7	4	9	81
420	12	8.1	3	9	81
540	11	6.1	10	1	1
660	10	5.8	12	2	4
780	9	6.2	8.5	0.5	0.25
900	8	7.2	6	2	4
1,020	7	7.5	5	2	4
1,120	6	6.2	8.5	2.5	6.25
1,220	5	6.5	7	2	4
1,340	4	5.8	12	8	64
1,460	3	4.8	15	12	144
1,580	2	5.0	14	12	144
1,700	1	5.8	12	11	121
					996.5

$$= 1 - \frac{5{,}979}{3{,}360}$$

$$= 1 - 1.78$$

$$= -0.78$$

The coefficient indicates that there is a negative relationship between the two sets of data — as the distance increases, the mean shingle diameter decreases.

The result is significant at the 0.01 significance level. The R_s value is greater than the critical value when $n = 15$ (0.63). The possibility that such a result occurred by chance is very low — less than 1 in 100.

This statistically reliable result supports the subjective perception of the longitudinal changes with distance from the southwest end of the beach.

Location quotients

A location quotient is a measure of the degree to which a geographical activity is concentrated in an area. As in the case of the Spearman rank correlation coefficient, the end product is a number, which again gives an objective value to use for comparison. The numerical value compares the concentration of an activity in a sub-region with the concentration in the whole region.

For example, when studying the concentration of employment in an industry in a particular region of a country, the calculation of the location quotient is:

$$LQ = \frac{X'/Y'}{X/Y}$$

where:
- X' is the number employed in the given industry in the region
- Y' is the number employed in all industries in that region
- X is the number employed in the given industry in the country as a whole
- Y is the number employed in all industries in that country

In this case the location quotient compares the proportion of employed people in a particular region in a given industry with the proportion in that industry nationally.

Sometimes data are given in percentage form, in which case the calculation is more straightforward.

$$LQ = \frac{(\%\ \text{of workers in the given activity in the region})}{(\%\ \text{of workers in the activity nationally})}$$

The key indicator in the use of location quotients is $LQ = 1.0$. A result of this nature would indicate that the region in question has a fair share of that geographical activity compared with the rest of the country. The relative proportions, region versus country, are equal.

If LQ > 1.0, this would indicate a greater share of that activity in the region compared with the rest of the country. In other words, there is a concentration of the activity in that region.

Similarly, if LQ < 1.0, the region has less than its proportionate share — the activity is under-represented.

Nearest neighbour statistic (R_n)

This statistic analyses the distribution of individual points in a pattern. It can be applied to the distribution of any data that can be plotted as point locations. Consequently, it is often used to analyse the distribution of shop types in a town centre, the distribution of various sizes of settlement in an area and the distribution of some public services, for example doctors' surgeries, in an urban area.

The basis of the statistic is the measurement of the distance between each point in a pattern and its nearest neighbour. This must be done for each point identified within the area studied. Once all measurements have been completed, the mean distance ($\bar{d}$) between each point should be calculated.

The nearest neighbour statistic can then be calculated using:

$$R_n = 2\bar{d}\sqrt{\frac{N}{A}}$$

where:
- N is the number of point locations in the area
- A is the area of study

The statistic can be any value between 0 and 2.15:
- 0 represents a pattern that is perfectly clustered, that is, there is no distance between nearest neighbours — all the points are at the same location. If this were the case, there would be no pattern to analyse.
- 2.15 represents a pattern displaying perfect regularity — all points lie at the vertices of equilateral triangles. All distances between nearest neighbours would be identical. Again this is highly unlikely in the real world.
- 1.0 is said to represent a random pattern, although this is difficult to prove.

In practice, the outcome of such a calculation will be on the continuum between 0 and 2.15. Proximity to one of these will indicate the degree of either clustering or regularity.

Requirements of the method

When carrying out a nearest neighbour statistic calculation, it is advisable to map the activity (or activities) first onto a transparent overlay. Using the overlay in the measurement and calculation process removes any potential distraction. Another requirement is that the units of measurement of distance and of area correspond, in most cases either metres and square metres, or kilometres and square kilometres.

A further complication is the delineation of the area to be studied. In the case of settlement-based work, you have to decide on the boundary of the area you are studying. You can then establish a buffer zone around this study area. If the nearest neighbour is within this buffer zone, you should measure *to* this point. However, this point in the buffer zone should not be counted in the overall study as a point *from* which to measure to its nearest neighbour. In short, you should only measure *to* points in the buffer zone, not *from* them.

The chi-squared test

This technique is used to assess the degree to which there are differences between a set of collected (or observed) data and a theoretical (or expected) set of data, together with the statistical significance of the differences.

The observed data are those that have been collected either in the field or from secondary sources. The expected data are those that would be expected according to the theoretical hypothesis being tested.

Using chi-squared

Normally, before the test is applied, it is necessary to formulate a null hypothesis. In the example given here, the null hypothesis would be that there is no significant difference between the observed and expected data distribution. The alternative to this would be that there is a difference between the observed and expected data, and that there is some factor responsible for this.

The method of calculating chi-squared is shown below. The letters A to D in Table 8 refer to the areas A to D in Figure 20. The column headed 'Observed (*O*)' lists the number of points in each of the areas A to D on Figure 20 (the *observed* frequencies). The total number of points in this case is 40. Column 'Expected (*E*)' contains the list of *expected* frequencies in each of the areas A to D assuming that the points are evenly spaced. In the column '*O* – *E*', each of the expected frequencies is subtracted from the observed frequencies, while in the last column '$(O - E)^2$' the result is squared. The relevant values are then inserted into the expression for chi-square, and the result is 4.0.

A B C D

Figure 20

Table 8

Map	Observed (O)	Expected (E)	O – E	(O – E)²
A	8	10	−2	4
B	14	10	4	16
C	6	10	−4	16
D	12	10	2	4
Sum	40	40	0	40

$$\chi^2 = \sum \frac{(O - E)^2}{E}$$

$$= \frac{40}{10}$$

$$= 4.0$$

The aim of a chi-squared test, therefore, is to find out whether the observed pattern agrees with or differs from the theoretical (expected) pattern. This can be measured by comparing the calculated result of the test with its level of significance.

To do this, the number of degrees of freedom must first be determined. This is done using the formula $(n - 1)$, where n is the number of observations, in this case the number of cells that contain observed data (4). So, $4 - 1 = 3$. Statistical tables give the distribution of chi-squared values for these degrees of freedom.

Then there are the levels of significance. There are two levels of significance: 95% and 99%. At 95% there is a 1 in 20 probability that the pattern being considered occurred by chance, and at 99% there is only a 1 in 100 probability that the pattern is one of chance. The levels of significance can be found in a book of statistical tables. They are also called confidence levels.

If the calculated value is the same as or greater than the values given in the table, the null hypothesis can be rejected and the alternative hypothesis accepted.

In the case of our example, however, the value of chi-squared is very low (4.0), showing that there is little difference between the observed and the expected pattern. The null hypothesis cannot therefore be rejected.

Some further points on this technique
▶ The numbers of both observed and expected values must be large enough to ensure that the test is valid. Most experts state there should be a minimum of five.

▶ The number produced by the calculation is itself meaningless. It is only of value when used in conjunction with statistical tables.

▶ Only significance (or confidence) levels of 95% and 99% should be considered when rejecting the null hypothesis (as in the case of the Spearman rank correlation coefficient). Any levels of confidence greater than these simply allow the null hypothesis to be rejected with even greater confidence.

▶ It is strongly recommended that you do not apply the test to more than one set of observed data, otherwise the mathematics become too complex.

The Mann–Whitney U test

To carry out the Mann–Whitney U test:
▶ set out the data in two columns
▶ rank each item of data in terms of its position within the sample as a whole; start with the lowest value
▶ add the ranks for each column
▶ calculate the value of U by using the formula:

$$U = n_1 n_2 + \frac{n_1(n_1 + 1)}{2} - \Sigma r_1$$

where:
n_1 and n_2 are the two sample sizes
Σr_1 is the sum of the ranks for sample 1

▶ using a table of critical values, interpret the answer that you have calculated

If the calculated value of U is less than or equal to the critical value at the chosen significance level, the null hypothesis must be rejected. The null hypothesis is that there is no significant difference between the two data sets. Therefore, if the null hypothesis is rejected, there is a difference.

Worked example: Mann–Whitney U test

An investigation was carried out into the effect of the sea on a beach in the west of England at different times of year. Two samples of pebbles were taken, one in April and the other in October. The hypothesis is that the mean size of the beach material will be larger in October than in April. Therefore, the null hypothesis is that there will be no difference.

The size categories (phi categories) that were used in the survey are shown in Table 9.

Calculation of U

The mean particle sizes at six sites in October and April were calculated. After ranking, the data were recorded in a table (Table 10).

Table 9 *Size categories of beach material*

Phi (Φ)	Particle diameter (mm)	Size category (Wentworth grade)	
−6.0	64.0	Cobbles	
−5.5	44.8		60.0 mm
−5.0	32.0	Coarse gravel	
−4.5	22.41		
−4.0	16.0		20.0 mm
−3.5	11.2	Medium gravel	
−3.0	8.0		
−2.5	5.6		6.0 mm
−2.0	4.0	Fine gravel	
−1.5	2.8		
−1.0	2.0		
−0.5	1.4		2.0 mm
0.0	1.0	Coarse sand	
0.5	0.71		
1.0	0.50		0.6 mm
1.5	0.355	Medium sand	
2.0	0.25		
2.5	0.18		0.2 mm
3.0	0.125	Fine sand	
3.5	0.090		
4.0	0.063		
			0.06 mm

Table 10 *Mean particle size and rank at six sites, October and April*

Site number	Mean particle size (using phi scale) in October (x)	Rank (r_x)	Mean particle size (using phi scale) in April (y)	Rank (r_y)
1	−2.506	5	−1.567	1
2	−2.483	4	−2.286	3
3	−2.612	7	−2.562	6
4	−2.726	8	−3.368	11
5	−3.281	10	−1.772	2
6	−3.394	12	−2.727	9
		$\Sigma r_x = 46$		$\Sigma r_y = 32$

U is calculated using the following formula:

$$U_x = n_x n_y + \frac{n_x(n_x + 1)}{2} - \Sigma r_x$$

$$= 36 + \frac{42}{2} - 46$$

$$= 11$$

$$U_y = n_x n_y + \frac{n_y(n_y + 1)}{2} - \Sigma r_y$$

$$= 36 + \frac{42}{2} - 32$$

$$= 25$$

where:

n_x and n_y are sample sizes

Σr_x and Σr_y are the sum of the rank values of r_x and r_y, respectively.

		Significance level	
Sample size		0.05	0.01
n_x	n_y		
6	6	7	3

Table 11 Critical values for the interpretation of the value of U

Once the value of U_x is established as 11, it is necessary to interpret this value (Table 11).

The value of 11 obtained for U_x clearly exceeds the critical value of 3 or 7. This means that the null hypothesis must be accepted; the proposed hypothesis must be rejected.

Therefore, there is no significant difference in beach material size in April and October; the size in October is not larger than that in April.

And finally...

It is important to note that all these techniques should be used only as a support for your own ideas on the geographical significance of your study. All results, and the statistical analysis of them, should be related to the original hypothesis and the established theory in that area of geography.

Your results may support established theory or your hypothesis, or they may not. If they do not, there may be some factor that is responsible that could lead to further studies. Above all, your investigation should make geograph-ical sense. This is far more important than demonstrating your ability to use mathematics or statistics.

The use of technology

You may wish to:
- use remotely sensed data — photographs and digital images, including those captured by satellite (note these provide only a snapshot image of the time when the image was taken)

- use databases, e.g. census data, Environment Agency data, Meteorological Office data
- use geographical information systems (GIS)
- present text and graphical and cartographical images using ICT

Geographical information systems (GIS)

Geographical information systems (GIS) are an integral part of twenty-first century geographical study. They are used extensively by environmental planners, government departments, public utility companies and commercial companies. GIS have the ability to store, retrieve, manipulate and analyse a wide range of spatially related data. They can:
- help with interrogating and understanding data
- enable multiple interrogation of complex data
- illustrate difficult abstract concepts in a dynamic visual way
- make use of three-dimensional representations
- provide opportunities for modelling and decision-making

GIS are an effective mapping tool and can be major elements in geographical fieldwork.

Figure 21 summarises the key aspects of GIS and how they can be used in fieldwork.

Figure 21
Maximising
the use of GIS
in fieldwork

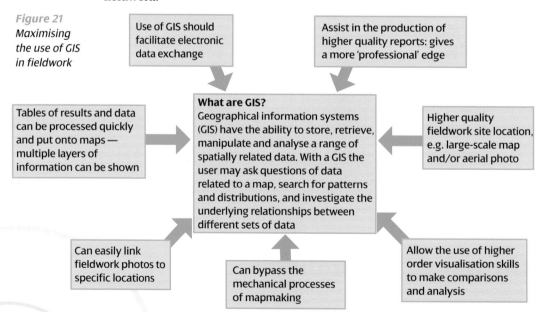

A number of websites and associated programs have great potential for use in fieldwork. They include Multimap, Aegis, Digital Worlds, Quikmaps and Google Earth. Many allow you to use maps and photos together; others allow annotations to be added. Some types of software require a degree of training whereas others are more straightforward to use. It all depends on your own level of ICT skills.

Global positioning systems (GPS) technology can also be useful in fieldwork. Data can be recorded at points along a transect or other sampling system, and the position of each point can be recorded at the same time. GPS-located data can then be fed into a GIS programme, bringing data recording and mapping together.

Writing up the report

You may be asked by your teacher to write up your completed enquiry for the examination that will follow. You may also want to submit it as part of the Extended Project Qualification (EPQ). Your report should be well structured, logically organised, and clearly and concisely written. There are three aspects to this process that you should consider: structure, language and presentation.

Structure

The structure should assist the reader in understanding the report and should also help you in organising it logically. The following checklist provides a generalised structure for your report:
▶ cover sheet
▶ title page and contents page
▶ executive summary (if required)
▶ aims and objectives
▶ scene setting (if required)
▶ research questions/hypotheses/issues being examined
▶ sources of information used
▶ methods of data collection, and commentary on their limitations
▶ data presentation, analysis and interpretation
▶ evaluation and conclusion
▶ bibliography and appendices

You need not attempt to write these in the order given. Indeed, it may be easier if you do not. For example, the executive summary is perhaps best written at the end of the whole process, as it is only at this stage that the complete picture can be described. What follows is a suggested order of completion.

1 Data presentation, analysis and interpretation
This is the section in which you present and analyse your findings. At this stage of your investigation you will have collected the data, sorted them and selected the most useful pieces. You will know what you have found out and

what it all means. Your results will be complete and they will be fresh in your mind. You should be able to interpret each separate section of your results and formulate conclusions for each one. The whole picture may begin to appear in your head.

2 Sources of information and methods of data collection

Now you can write about what information you collected and how you did so. Do not forget to discuss any limitations of the methods of collection that you used, or of the data sources themselves.

3 Conclusion and evaluation

This should include a summary of all the major findings of your investigation and an evaluation of them. Do not present anything new to the reader at this stage. Towards the end of this section, try to draw together the sub-conclusions from each section of the data analysis into one overall conclusion — the whole picture.

4 Aims, objectives, research questions and scene setting (introduction)

Having written up the bulk of the investigation, you can now write the intro-duction, making sure it ties in with what follows it. This section should acquaint the reader with the purpose of the investigation and the background to it.

5 Appendices and bibliography

The appendices contain additional supplementary evidence that may be of interest to the reader but is not essential to the main findings. The bibliog-raphy provides details of the secondary sources that have been used in your research, either as guides or as sources of information. You should give the author, date of publication, title of the publication, publisher and page number. If you use direct quotes in the body of your report, you should provide the name of the author and date of publication in the text, and cross-refer it back to the bibliography.

6 Contents page

All sections of the report should be listed in sequence, with accurate page references.

7 Title page

This should state the title of your report, your name and any other informa-tion required by your school.

8 Executive summary

An executive summary should be a brief statement, no more than 250 words in length, covering all the main aspects of the investigation. A good executive summary introduces the subject of the full report, refers to its aims and objectives, and provides a brief synopsis of the findings. A very good

executive summary will tempt the reader into wanting to read more by being comprehensible, interesting and stimulating. It should also make sense and read as a separate document from the full report.

Language

The quality of language that you use in the writing up of your investigation is important. You are in complete control of this aspect of the process, and your style of writing must be appropriate for this exercise. You should avoid poor use of English and try to maintain accuracy at all times. In particular:
- your sentences should be grammatically correct and well punctuated
- your writing should be well structured, with good use of paragraphs
- your spelling must be accurate (use a dictionary and PC spellcheck)
- you must be clear in your use of specialist terminology and in the expression of your ideas
- you should be aware that the assessment of your work will take into account the above aspects of your writing

Proofreading is an important part of this process. Prior to submission, make sure you read through the draft from start to finish and mark any places where there are errors or inconsistencies. If possible, get someone to do this for you; parents are often useful in this respect. It must be someone who is going to be highly critical of what you have written.

Another key checking stage is making sure that maps and diagrams are located in the correct place — it is irritating for the reader to flick backwards and forwards when trying to read a report of this type. Make sure all the references in the text are included in the bibliography.

Presentation

It is a fact of life that most people are influenced by presentation. Bear in mind the following:
- A neatly presented handwritten or word-processed report will create a favourable impression before the content is read.
- Adequate heading and numbering of pages, with carefully produced illustrations, will make it easier for the reader to understand what is contained within the report.
- Layout is also important. Do not crowd the pages with dense text, which looks unattractive. Provide adequate margins, use either double or 1.5 line spacing in word-processing and make use of clear heading levels, with short paragraphs.

You should now be in a position to submit your finished product, confident in the belief that it is the best you could have done.

Logarithmic graph paper

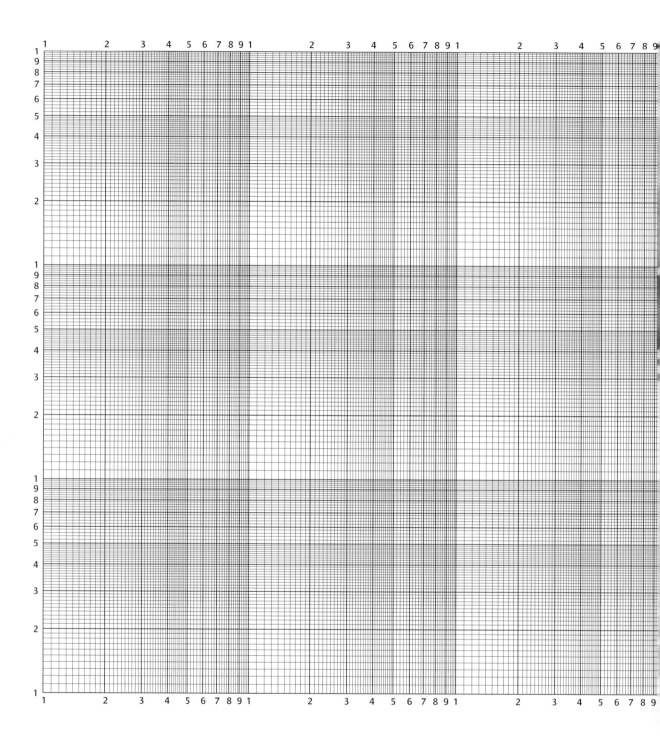

Semi-logarithmic graph paper

Triangular graph paper

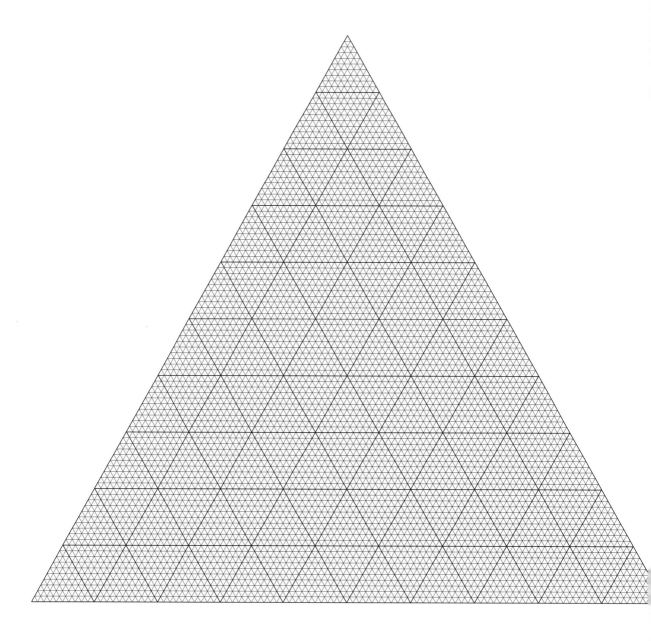

Written examinations

The first section of this book examines the processes involved in completing and writing up a geographical investigation, in preparation for a written examination. The written examinations offered by the various A-level examination boards are different. This section looks at the requirements of the written examinations as set by AQA, Edexcel and OCR. Example questions are given for each board, together with commentary (indicated by 🖉) and sample mark schemes. The summary requirements for each of the boards is given in Table 1 on page 3.

The AQA specification

In the AQA specification there are three elements to the assessment of geographical investigative and research skills:
▶ at AS Unit 2 (Geographical skills), which carries 15% of the A-level award
▶ at A2 either Unit 4A (Geography fieldwork investigation) or Unit 4B (Geographical issue evaluation), each of which accounts for 20% of the A-level award

Unit 2 Geographical skills

In this examination, which is 1 hour in length, there are two compulsory questions, each carrying 25 marks.

Question 1 (which is skills based) is always set in the context of one of the two core topics: Rivers, floods and management, or Population change, with no pattern to their order. The questions here test a range of skills, such as photograph interpretation (including satellite imagery), map work, presentation techniques, graphical techniques, statistical techniques and text comprehension.

These skills are described in the first section of this book, and therefore will not be looked at further here.

Question 2 relates specifically to the fieldwork and investigative research you have undertaken. This fieldwork must be based on an aspect of the content of Unit 1 — Rivers, floods and management, Cold environments, Coastal environments, Hot desert environments and their margins, Population change, Food supply issues, Energy issues or Health issues.

Note that this is the *only* restriction on the nature of your fieldwork — it is possible for you to base your fieldwork on an option that you have not studied.

A range of possible questions that may be asked, together with guidance on how to answer them, is given below.

Example questions
All the questions are likely to begin with a 'stem' such as:

You have experience of geography fieldwork as part of your course...

or

With reference to a piece of fieldwork you have recently undertaken...

All parts of the question will relate to this stem.

Example question 1

a **Briefly outline its aim, and state one hypothesis you sought to test.**
(3 marks)

e The basic aim of an enquiry could be to assess the quality of provision of services in an area of rural settlement. You might then go on to state the hypothesis that the provision was sufficient for the local population's needs.

One mark for basic statement of aims, 1 mark for hypothesis and 1 mark for the linkage between the two, to max 3.

b **For your chosen study, identify one item of primary data which was collected. Briefly state how it was collected and give reasons for adopting the method described.** (7 marks)

e For the survey in a village mentioned in (a), a questionnaire may have been used. Sampling could have been carried out on a systematic basis, interviewing people in the street, and by using a 'drop and collect' method. The questionnaire would have used a mixture of closed and open questions. This would cover the entire village so a picture would emerge that was representative of the village as a whole. It would have been difficult to carry out stratified sampling without knowing the make-up of each household.

Level 1   Simple statements of data collection methodology, possibly including the sampling strategy. Weak statements of rationale/justification.
(1–4 marks)

Level 2 Detailed statements of data collection strategy – the examiner has a clear sense of how the data collection was done. Appropriate statements of justification. To attain the highest marks, all elements must be answered to this standard. (5–7 marks)

c **Before visiting an area for fieldwork, a risk assessment must be completed. State one risk associated with carrying out fieldwork in the study area and suggest how you would minimise the risk.** (3 marks)

🖉 Risks may include (and how to minimise the risk):
▶ traffic hazards on narrow lanes/roads (face oncoming traffic, walk in single file)
▶ risk of offending people (be polite at all times, have an appropriate introduction)

One mark for each valid statement to max 3.

d **Stating the results of your investigation, explain how they helped to improve your understanding of the topic or environment investigated.** (7 marks)

🖉 In general terms, you are expected to make some reference to your results and to make comments on how these added to your understanding, perhaps in relation to established theory or in an analysis and evaluation of anomalies.

Level 1 Answer is at a basic level; general advantages of fieldwork, e.g. 'seeing things for yourself'. (1–4 marks)

Level 2 A clear indication as to how a specified result added to understanding; clear support for general theory or recognition of anomalies and further discussion. (5–7 marks)

e **Describe one application of ICT skills in carrying out your fieldwork and comment on its usefulness.** (5 marks)

🖉 Use of the internet could have allowed maps at a variety of scales to be identified prior to the visit and enabled the area to be put into context, providing base maps of streets. The website **www.multimap.co.uk** could be searched. Maps at a variety of scales can be downloaded and printed off.

Level 1 Brief statements of application – use of internet – and simple statements of how it was used. No real commentary of usefulness. (1–3 marks)

Level 2 More detailed/sophisticated statements of application, perhaps giving details of a website. Detailed commentary on the value of that application. (4–5 marks)

Example question 2

a   Outline the aim, one objective and the theory/concepts that provided the idea for study.   (3 marks)

e *Aim:* Any small-scale stated aim is valid. For example: 'Is there evidence of succession along a transect in the sand dunes at X?'

Objective: For the sand dune example, the objective could be to determine whether the amount of vegetation cover changes with distance from the high water mark.

Theory/concept: For the sand dune example, a valid theory/concept could be a psammosere, which predicts changes in vegetation cover and diversity.

One mark for each of aim, objective and theory/concept, to max 3.

b   Outline one source of information that you used and assess the extent to which it was 'fit for purpose'.   (3 marks)

e One source of information that could be used prior to the investigation is photographs across the area inland from the sea. These would show evidence of changes in vegetation amount and type. A concern here is your ability to identify species, but as it stands at the moment only the amount of vegetation cover is being studied.

One mark for each valid statement to max 3.

c   For your chosen study, identify one item of primary data that was collected. Outline the method of collection and how one risk related to this collection was minimised.   (5 marks)

e For the psammosere example, the item of primary data could be the amount of vegetation cover along the transect.

The ways in which the data were collected could include:
▶   quadrats placed every 10 m along a transect beginning at the HWM
▶   the proportion of vegetation cover determined by counting the squares within the quadrat

Risks include getting lost within the area and the weather, which can be extremely wet in coastal areas in the UK. Risks could be reduced by:
▶   use of a compass together with a detailed map of the area
▶   appropriate waterproof clothing and boots/footwear

Level 1   Simple statements of data collection methodology. Weak statements of risk management.   (1–3 marks)

Level 2   Detailed statements of data collection/sampling strategy – the examiner has a clear sense of how the data collection was done. Appropriate statements of risk management.   (4–5 marks) d **Describe a method of presentation that you used in your investigation and indicate how the chosen method was useful.** (7 marks)

🖊 In general terms, the method should be described clearly in the context of the study, and you should indicate the nature of the data that are being presented. Some reasoning for using this method should be clear in terms of 'being useful', perhaps because it allowed clear patterns to be observed or some form of analysis to be undertaken, albeit at a fairly superficial or subjective level.

Level 1 Describes method without reference to its usefulness. (1–4 marks)

Level 2 Clear indication of the method of presentation or developed reference to show how technique was useful. Some indication as to why the method was chosen — expands on 'useful'. (5–7 marks)

e **Stating the results of your investigation, explain how they helped to improve your understanding of the topic or environment investigated.** (7 marks)

🖊 You are expected to make some reference to your results and to comment on how these helped your understanding, perhaps in relation to established theory or in an analysis and evaluation of anomalies.

Level 1 Answer is at a basic level; general advantages of fieldwork, e.g. 'seeing things for yourself'. (1–4 marks)

Level 2 A clear indication as to how a specified result added to understanding; clear support for general theory or recognition of anomalies and further discussion. (5–7 marks)

Example question 3

a **Explain how you devised your aim and how you responded to the risks associated with your chosen site for fieldwork.** (8 marks)

🖊 The aim should be clearly linked to an achievable outcome and realistic in terms of geographical scale and/or timescale. You should give a clear statement of the location of your fieldwork. You are expected to identify more than one risk associated with this location and give a clear account of how you managed those risks.

Level 1 A basic grasp/statement of aim. No/weak reference to underpinning theory of the aim. The answer does not give a clear set of statements regarding risks, or any sense of risk assessment. Risks and responses to them are general, and not related to the specific site chosen. (1–4 marks)

Level 2 Clear and appropriate aim stated, with clear links to underpinning theory. Risks are clearly outlined, and there is a clear sense that the student has experienced the process of risk assessment. Responses to risk are thoughtful, considered and appropriate   (5–8 marks)

b **Outline and justify the data collection method for one of your methodologies.**   (6 marks)

✍ Any data collection method is acceptable providing you make clear reference to the suitability/appropriateness in relation to the data being collected. This is the justification. Collecting secondary data is also acceptable. Answers that refer to data collection methods that are inappropriate to the nature of the data will be held within Level 1.

Level 1 Data collection method is named but outlined in a simplistic manner. The justification is generic or even inappropriate.   (1–4 marks)

Level 2 Data collection technique is appropriate for the data collected, and is outlined in detail and with clarity. The justification is specific to the nature of data collected.   (5–6 marks)

c **Describe and illustrate one technique you used to present data in this enquiry.**   (6 marks)

✍ The description and illustration must link to each other and be appropriate for the data collected. Any technique is acceptable providing you link it to the theme of the enquiry. A sketch (an illustration) is required by the question, and answers that do not contain such a sketch will remain within Level 1. Good-quality annotations may be used or, alternatively, you can describe the sketch in the text.

Level 1 Simplistic identification/description of a technique which may contain errors or omissions. The description is lacking in detail — consists of simple statements. The illustration is equally simplistic, and may be general.   (1–4 marks)

Level 2 Detailed description of the method, illustrated with a clear sketch/diagram. The method is appropriate for the enquiry.   (5–6 marks)

d **Making specific reference to your results, summarise your findings and suggest how this enquiry could be improved.**   (5 marks)

✍ You should refer to actual results and findings that you developed. The findings should relate to the aim of the enquiry as given in (a). You should then make clear statements as to how the enquiry could have been improved, most likely in terms of the methodology. The suggested improvement should be realistic and logical, with reference to some element of limitation of the original enquiry.

Level 1 Very basic concluding statements which have a loose connection to the aims of the enquiry, and may be general. There is a lack of specific detail in terms of actual results. Statements of improvement are either absent or simplistic. No explanation as to how improvement could be made. (1–3 marks)

Level 2 Concluding statements make good use of data to support and record findings, with the possible identification of anomalous results. Improvement is elaborated upon to show how change(s) would impact on the enquiry. (4–5 marks)

Example question 4

a **Describe the location of your fieldwork and explain why it was suitable for your investigation.** (4 marks)

🄮 You should state precisely where your fieldwork was based and the nature of the environment in which it was based. For example, for fieldwork on a cold environment, you could have studied the Llanberis Pass, which exhibits a range of glacial landforms. Justification of the site requires you to give some detail as to why that location is suitable for the factor you are seeking to investigate — you could relate the location to either the aim or a hypothesis.

Up to 2 marks for the location of the fieldwork, and 2 marks for the justification, to a maximum of 4 marks.

b **Outline one hypothesis and describe one methodology for primary data collection in relation to this.** (5 marks)

🄮 This type of question has been covered earlier — see similar questions above.

c **Examine the limitations of your chosen methodology.** (6 marks)

🄮 You are expected to explore the limitations of your chosen method of data collection, and indeed of other techniques. This is an important aspect of evaluating investigative work. It is recommended that you reflect on limitations as soon as you can after undertaking any technique.

Level 1 A simplistic awareness of limitations. Answer tends to concentrate on difficulties of implementing the technique rather than as to why the technique may have been inappropriate at the outset. (1–4 marks)

Level 2 A more detailed and sophisticated response which demonstrates an understanding of the limitations in the context of the enquiry. Some reference to the choice of technique as well as its implementation. (5–6 marks) d **Outline and justify the use of one technique to statistically analyse your results.** (5 marks)

🖉 You could use any technique from within the specification, including those identified for A2. Be sure that you refer to a technique that requires some manipulation of the data statistically, and not in a diagrammatic or graphical form.

Level 1 A simplistic response which describes the nature of the technique but provides little detail as to how it can be used. There is little sense the student used this technique — the answer is generic. There is little or no justification. (1–3 marks)

Level 2 A detailed response which describes the technique clearly with clear reference to actual data used. Justification is clear and relates to the benefits/appropriateness of the technique in relation to the data collected. (4–5 marks)

e **Drawing upon your findings, explain how your enquiry improved your understanding of the topic area.** (5 marks)

🖉 This type of question has been covered earlier — see similar questions above.

Unit 4

You have an optional route at A2, either:
▶ **Unit 4A** (Geography fieldwork investigation), or
▶ **Unit 4B** (Geographical issue evaluation)

Both of these papers are $1\frac{1}{2}$ hours in length and carry 60 marks.

Unit 4A has two sections. **Section A** (40 marks) assesses a personal fieldwork investigation that you have undertaken with the broad task of:

the individual investigation of a geographical argument, assertion, hypothesis, issue or problem.

There are no restrictions on the type of topic that can be studied other than it should be geographical and include primary, and where relevant secondary, data collection, should be based on a small area of study and be linked to the content of the specification. This is a very wide brief. It is also clear that this investigation/fieldwork must be completed at a level above that done at AS.

Section B (20 marks) assesses fieldwork and investigative and research skills on material that is unfamiliar to you. Questions are set involving data, skills and techniques used in presentation and analysis to enable you to interpret, analyse and evaluate geographical information and apply understanding in unfamiliar contexts. These skills are described in the first section of this book, and therefore will not be looked at further in this section.

Unit 4B is a geographical issue evaluation exercise. It essentially assesses the skills of issue evaluation, which are not the subject of this book. However, within the tasks there are some questions relating to data gathering (including fieldwork), presentation and analysis. You will be tested on your ability to apply understanding in unfamiliar contexts using fieldwork-based stimulus material. As with Unit 4A Section B, these skills are described in the first section of this book, and therefore will not be looked at further here.

What follows, therefore, is an examination of the range of possible questions that may be asked in **Unit 4A Section A**, together with guidance on how to answer them.

Example questions

As in Unit 2 at AS, all the questions are likely to begin with a 'stem' such as:

You have experience of geography fieldwork as part of your course...

or

With reference to a piece of fieldwork you have recently undertaken...

All parts of the question will then relate to this stem.

Example question 1

a **Explain why the location of your fieldwork was appropriate for the investigation.** (12 marks)

📝 Two elements are required for a response to this question: the location and its suitability for the investigation. The underpinning theory should be linked to the specification; hence, the location is expected to be suitable to investigate the aims and, by implication, the theory. So, in your answer make sure you link theory > location > investigation > theory.

Level 1   The candidate is unable to set out the aims in full; much confusion may be apparent at the lower end of the band. Towards the upper end of the band, there may be background of relevance to the location, but not linked to the aims. Alternatively, the aims may be justified but there is limited reference to the location. There will be little reference to the candidate's own fieldwork investigation at the upper end, while this will be absent at the lower end of the mark band. (1–4 marks)

Level 2 There will be clear reference to both location and aims, but there is likely to be an imbalance. This will be very marked at the lower end, perhaps with implicit links, whereas at the upper end the imbalance will be less and there will be reference to the appropriateness of the location. There will be some reference to the fieldwork undertaken, increasing up through the band. (5–8 marks)

Level 3 There will be detailed reference to both location and aims and this will be consistently integrated to demonstrate the appropriateness of the location for the investigation. There will be detailed and increasingly convincing reference to the fieldwork undertaken. (9–12 marks)

b **(i) Assess the usefulness of one method used to collect data for the investigation.** (6 marks)

🄴 The method selected must relate to the investigation. Only one method is required. Any appropriate method is acceptable. The methods are detailed in the first part of this book.

Level 1 There is likely to be a description of the method selected. This will be basic at the lower end, more structured at the upper end of the band. There will be no reference to the fieldwork undertaken at the lower end, with some, perhaps basic, reference at the upper end of the band. There will be little, if any, attempt to assess the usefulness of the method selected. (1–4 marks)

Level 2 There will be a clear assessment of the usefulness of the method selected. There will be increasing rigour demonstrated. There will be increasingly clear and convincing reference to the fieldwork undertaken. (5–6 marks)

b **(ii) Analyse the strengths and limitations of this method in meeting the aim of your investigation.** (12 marks)

🄴 Any relevant method can be used, but it must be that selected in (i). Reference to strengths, limitations and a link to the aim of the specific investigation is expected.

Level 1 There will be a basic awareness of strengths and limitations of the method selected. There is likely to be a strong focus on either strengths or limitations. There is likely to be a straightforward use of expression. Reference to any data collection method used will be basic, if present. There will be basic reference to the aims of the investigation and the candidate's own fieldwork experience is unlikely to be mentioned. (1–4 marks)

Level 2 There will be clear reference to both strengths and limitations, but there is likely to be an imbalance. This will be very marked at the lower end, perhaps with implicit links, whereas at the upper end the imbalance will be less and there will be clear reference to the aims of the investigation and the fieldwork experience undertaken, increasing up through the band. A clear reference to any data collection method used is expected. (5–8 marks)

Level 3 There will be detailed reference to analyse both strengths and limitations and this will be consistently referenced to the aims of the investigation. A detailed commentary on the suitability of any data collection method used is expected. There will be detailed and increasingly convincing reference to the fieldwork undertaken. (9–12 marks)

c **Evaluate your investigation in the light of its aim and underpinning geographical theory.** (10 marks)

    ✏ You should make reference to the aim and underpinning theory as set out in (a). Evaluation of the investigation as a whole is expected, in the light of the fieldwork experience.

Level 1 There will be basic awareness of the conclusions gained from the investigation. There is likely to be a strong focus on the conclusions, rather than any evaluation. There is likely to be a straightforward use of expression. There will be a basic or no reference to the aim of the investigation and the underpinning geographical theory in the light of the candidate's own fieldwork experience. (1–4 marks)

Level 2 There will be clear reference to both the conclusions and evaluation of the investigation, but there is likely to be an imbalance. This will be more apparent at the lower end, perhaps with implicit links, whereas, at the upper end, the imbalance will be less and there will be clear reference to the aim of the investigation and the underpinning geographical theory. A clear reference to the fieldwork experience undertaken, increasing up through the band, is expected. (5–8 marks)

Level 3 There will be detailed reference to the conclusions and there will be a meaningful evaluative theme. This will be consistently referenced to the aim of the investigation and the underpinning geographical theory. There will be detailed and increasingly convincing reference to the fieldwork undertaken. (9–10 marks)

Example question 2

a **Explain how your hypotheses/research questions evolved from the overall aim.** (5 marks)

ⓔ The difference between an aim and hypotheses/research questions should be clear in your mind. These are explained in the first part of this book. Note that at A-level it is better to have more than one hypothesis/research question.

Level 1 Overall statement of aim given, together with a brief statement of hypothesis/research question. The links between the two are not well stated or made clear. (1–3 marks)

Level 2 Clear aim with statements of clear hypotheses/research questions, together with clear and logical link between them.

(4–5 marks)

b **How did you assess the safety issues associated with your enquiry?**
(5 marks)

ⓔ This question assesses the degree to which risk assessment has taken place. The precise nature of the assessment will depend on the nature and location of the fieldwork undertaken. Risk assessment is an important element of fieldwork and should form part of your preparatory processes.

Level 1 Simple statements of risk and of risk assessment. The answer could apply to any piece of fieldwork, there being no sense of appropriateness to the fieldwork being undertaken. (1–3 marks)

Level 2 Clear and precise statements of risk and of risk assessment. There is a clear sense of preparation prior to the fieldwork being undertaken, and being appropriate to the investigation undertaken.

(4–5 marks)

c **Describe the use you made of modern technology in either data collection or presentation and assess its value.** (10 marks)

ⓔ Clear evidence of the use of modern technology will be credited at a high level. There must be clear and detailed description of how the modern technology was used rather than the technology itself. Evidence of application of the technology to data collection or data presentation should be made clear. A strong answer will provide an indication of the benefits of using modern technology compared with not using it. An assessment of its value should include some evidence linked to the fieldwork undertaken, rather than generic information.

Level 1 Candidates offer limited description of the technology used, which may be combined with limited assessment of value. Tends to be generic rather than linked to fieldwork across AS and A2 at bottom of level. (1–4 marks)

Level 2 Description of use of technology combined with assessment of value but partially related to fieldwork. Competent description but no assessment of value or vice versa. Answer may have poor structure with some inaccurate spelling and inaccurate use of geographical terminology.

(5–8 marks)

Level 3 All aspects of indicative content covered in a fieldwork-focused context. Well-structured answers with accurate use of geographical terminology.

(9–10 marks)

d **Assess one method that you used to analyse your data. Explain why this method was suitable for your purposes.** (8 marks)

🖉 The method selected must relate to the investigation. Only one method is required. Any appropriate method is acceptable. The methods are detailed in the first part of this book.

Level 1 There is likely to be a description of the method selected. This will be basic at the lower end, more structured at the upper end of the band. There will be no reference to the fieldwork undertaken at the lower end, with some, perhaps basic, reference at the upper end of the band. There will be little, if any, attempt to assess the usefulness of the method selected.

(1–4 marks)

Level 2 There will be a clear assessment of the usefulness of the method selected. There will be increasing rigour demonstrated. There will be increasingly clear and convincing reference to the fieldwork undertaken.

(5–8 marks)

e **Explain how your investigation helped you to gain an understanding of the topic or the environment you were studying.** (12 marks)

🖉 You should make reference to the aim and hypotheses/research questions as set out in (a). Evaluation of the investigation as a whole is expected, in the light of the fieldwork experience.

Level 1 There will be basic awareness of the conclusions gained from the investigation. There is likely to be a strong focus on the conclusions, rather than any evaluation. There is likely to be a straightforward use of expression. There will be a basic or no reference to the aim of the investigation and the underpinning geographical theory/environment in the light of the candidate's own fieldwork experience.

(1–4 marks)

Level 2 There will be clear reference to both the conclusions and evaluation of the investigation, but there is likely to be an imbalance. This will be more apparent at the lower end, perhaps with implicit links, whereas, at the upper end, the imbalance will be less and there will be clear reference to the aim of the investigation and the underpinning geographical theory/environment. A clear reference to the fieldwork experience undertaken, increasing up through the band, is expected.

(5–8 marks)

Level 3 There will be detailed reference to the conclusions and there will be a meaningful evaluative theme. This will be consistently referenced to the aim of the investigation and the underpinning geographical theory/environment. There will be detailed and increasingly convincing reference to the fieldwork undertaken. (9–12 marks)

The Edexcel specification

In the Edexcel specification there are two elements to the assessment of geographical investigative and research skills:
▶ at AS Unit 2
▶ at A2 Unit 4

Each of these accounts for 20% of the A-level award — 40% in total.

Unit 2 Geographical investigations

You must choose one physical topic and one human topic from a choice of four:
▶ physical: either Extreme weather or Crowded coasts
▶ human: either Unequal spaces or Rebranding places

The examination paper is 1 hour in length; you must answer two questions, each carrying a total of 35 marks. Within each set of questions there are three parts: (a) data response; (b) management and impact issues; (c) investigation and evaluation skills. Fieldwork, research and practical work are all seen as part of this investigation process. They form an intrinsic part of each of these topics and this is reflected in the assessment process — questions on various parts of the geographical enquiry sequence carrying 15 of the 35 marks available. You are encouraged to look at issues on a small or local scale, relating these to your own life and experiences as well as comparing your research areas with a wider world context.

You are also required to use a resource booklet for the data response element, together with your own ideas and relevant fieldwork and research that you have carried out. You are not allowed to take any materials into the examination room.

Here we will look only at those questions that deal with the investigative aspect, that is, part (c), on a topic-by-topic basis.

Topic 1 Extreme weather

Fieldwork opportunities can include:

▶ a weather log
▶ a flood impact survey
▶ flood or drought risk assessments, based on either natural causes, e.g. meteorological, or human causes, e.g. changes resulting from urbanisation
▶ flood management assessments

Research work could include:

▶ weather records over time including synoptic charts
▶ satellite images over time and space
▶ data on the social, economic and environmental impact of tornadoes, hurricanes, floods
▶ the interpretation of statistics for significant flood/drought/heatwave events
▶ evaluations of various management strategies of extreme weather events

Topic 2 Crowded coasts

Fieldwork opportunities can include:

▶ surveys of coastal development and land use
▶ assessing the pressures of development on a coastline, such as pollution levels and destruction of habitats
▶ assessing the degree of coastal flood risk and the likely impact on development and people
▶ coastal management strategies, including assessing the success of coastal defence schemes
▶ assessing the state of the coastal environment

Research work could include:

▶ comparing satellite images to show coastal change
▶ using maps to show rates and extent of coastal erosion
▶ analysis of shoreline management schemes
▶ the interpretation of statistics for coastal retreat and flooding

Topic 3 Unequal spaces

Fieldwork opportunities can include:

▶ local environmental and housing quality surveys to explore the pattern of spatial inequality
▶ investigating the disparity of crime and vandalism

- assessing access to services
- looking at issues of mobility, especially in rural areas, e.g. in relation to emergency services, travel, shopping and education
- the evaluation of the success of schemes to tackle or address inequality, e.g. self-help schemes, public transport schemes, town planning initiatives, policing

Research work could include:

- surveys into the causes of inequality through questionnaires and interviews
- evaluation of schemes to address inequality
- the use of census data to show patterns of disparity and inequality
- the use of maps, statistics, planning documents and photographs to evaluate decline or improvement
- rural work could involve applying a modern day Cloke's Index (e.g. broadband access, mobile services, post offices)

Topic 4 Rebranding places

Fieldwork opportunities can include:

- the study of contrasting places in both rural and urban areas in terms of shopping, commercial and residential areas
- the evaluation of flagship schemes of redevelopment and gentrification of parts of urban areas
- examining the roles of sport and leisure, and tourism as catalysts for change
- surveys on housing quality and street furniture quality
- an urban tour — examining redevelopments and economic changes
- investigations into heritage (rural or urban) projects, e.g. arts and media projects, new rural technologies and rural diversification

Research work could include:

- reviewing websites of redevelopment schemes
- investigation of census data, e.g. inward migration of certain socio-economic groups, health, employment, housing tenure

The following example questions examine those aspects of the assessment relating to fieldwork and research in Unit 2. All questions carry 15 marks.

Example questions: Extreme weather

1 **Describe and explain a programme of fieldwork and research you would use to investigate the links between precipitation and flooding along a stretch of river.**

e Answers should focus on the planning and methodology of fieldwork and the use of research sources, and show how these link precipitation data to flood response. A weather diary over a number of days could record the amount and

intensity of rain or snowfall. In addition to this primary source, support could come from local or Meteorological Office data. Forecasts and newspapers would refer to the wider situation and antecedent conditions.

River flow data could be collected by fieldwork measurements, extrapolating discharge values for a river at flood level. Research could come from previous flood episodes as well as newspaper coverage or Environment Agency sources.

One of the simplest ways to see the links between rainfall input and flood response is by the flood, or storm, hydrograph, which plots rainfall against river discharge over time. It gives a clear picture of the river response and the likelihood of floods occurring.

Information about the amount and speed of surface runoff is a key factor, therefore infiltration rates, gradients, vegetation interception and channel geometry are also useful data. Obtaining these is likely to involve fieldwork rather than research. However, calculations such as flood return interval or flood frequency need reliable longer-term data to be useful, and you may have problems accessing such information.

2 **Describe the results of your fieldwork and research into the management schemes of extreme weather events, and explain how these helped you judge their effectiveness.**

🖉 Answers should focus on the results of an investigation into extreme weather events and their management, involving fieldwork and other sources, and how these can help assess their effectiveness.

Primary and secondary sources can be used to investigate management strategies, such as hurricane warning systems (e.g. FEMA and NOAA in the USA), Meteorological Office data, Environment Agency flood protection and risk assessment schemes. Research into the role of technology such as satellite imagery, community preparedness and forecasting systems, and its application to extreme weather management could be undertaken.

One approach could be to examine both short- and longer-term strategies of response, as well as to look at how strategies in some areas have changed over time.

The judgement of effectiveness requires both 'before' and 'after' commentary, or the use of a technique to show the positive and negative views of change. An analytical technique, e.g. a risk assessment or cost–benefit exercise, could be used.

Example questions: Crowded coasts

1 **Describe and explain a programme of fieldwork and research you would use to investigate the impacts of either coastal erosion or coastal flooding along a stretch of coastline.**

🖉 Answers should focus on the planning and methodology of fieldwork and the use of research sources to investigate the impacts of coastal erosion or flooding. Rates of erosion/flooding can be measured using secondary data, such as old photos, OS maps, records or newspapers. The Environment Agency and the Department for Environment Food and Rural Affairs (DEFRA) also measure and record information regularly, as do local councils.

A fieldwork snapshot of erosion or wave processes may establish likely causes. Surveys of the presence and state of repair of sea defences or protection schemes may indicate rates or impacts of erosion and flooding. The surveying of landslides/slumping, rockfalls and cliff face features is useful too.

Impacts involve consideration of land use and values, the amount of development and population density of the area being studied. This may need land-use surveys and research into rateable values to establish the degree and likelihood of risks, and perhaps an examination of hazard assessment.

Questionnaires to test the perceptions and concerns of local groups may be useful. Engineering consultants may have carried out research and could be approached.

2 **Describe the results of your fieldwork and research into coastal management schemes, and explain how these helped you judge their effectiveness.**

🄴 Answers should focus on the results of an investigation into coastal erosion and/or flooding events and their management, involving fieldwork and other sources, and give an explanation of how these results can help assess the effectiveness of the management schemes.

Primary and secondary sources can be used to investigate management strategies. You can, for example, map and record structures and their effectiveness as defences in coping with waves, longshore drift, storms, tides and flood levels. Data can be obtained from the Environment Agency and DEFRA, as well as from historical documents, maps, satellite images and university websites.

A number of coastal management strategies exist, ranging from hard engineering to soft engineering to 'do nothing'. Consideration of any of these schemes would be relevant. One approach could be to examine both short- and longer-term strategies of response, as well as to look at how strategies in some areas have changed over time.

The judgement of effectiveness requires both 'before' and 'after' commentary, or the use of a technique to show the positive and negative views of change, perhaps using an analytical technique, e.g. a cost–benefit or environmental impact exercise.

Example questions: Unequal spaces

1 **Describe the results of your fieldwork and research into how to reduce inequality, and explain how these help you to judge the success of either the urban or rural schemes involved.**

🖉 Answers should focus on the results of an investigation into urban or rural inequality, involving fieldwork and other sources, and how they can help assess the improvements involved.

Outcomes could include the number of jobs created and new businesses started, and improved socioeconomic or environmental conditions (e.g. going up-market, house improvement, filtering, environmental quality improvements, new building/fabric, provision of services, higher occupancy rates etc.)

Research into, and secondary data based on, rateable value changes, photographs, council/planning data and census data, e.g. population and employment structure, would be helpful. Additional data could come from groups such as Shelter, university researchers and other interest groups.

The judgement of success requires both 'before' and 'after' commentary, or the use of a technique to show the positive and negative views of change, perhaps using an analytical technique, e.g. a deprivation index.

2   **Describe and explain a programme of fieldwork and research you would use to investigate the impacts of inequality in either a rural area or an urban area.**

🖉 Answers should focus on the planning and methodology of fieldwork and the use of research sources to investigate the impacts of inequality in the chosen area.

The impacts of reduced opportunities and facilities, for example in deprived areas of inner cities, peripheral estates or remote rural areas, could be investigated. Effects of inequality may manifest themselves in measurable features, such as profiles of gender, age, ethnicity, education levels, income and health. The census and other websites can provide data for the basis of an investigation. Qualitative surveys and perception studies can also be used. The latter can be used to explore the notion of neighbourhood identity. A variety of different indicators can be used — social (car ownership, purchasing power), economic (employment type and quantity) and environmental (litter, cleanliness, green spaces).

Questionnaires to test the perceptions and concerns of local people and groups may be useful to determine the degree to which exclusion and polarisation has taken place.

Example questions: Rebranding places

1   **Describe the results of your fieldwork and research into how to evaluate urban rebranding, and explain how these help you to judge the success of the schemes involved.**

🖉 Answers should focus on the results of an investigation into urban rebranding, involving fieldwork and other sources, and how these can help assess the success of such schemes. Flagship schemes, gentrification, sport and leisure provision are all suitable target schemes.

Outcomes could include the number of jobs created and new businesses started, and improved socioeconomic or environmental conditions (e.g. going up-market, house improvement, filtering, environmental quality improvements, new building/fabric, provision of services, higher occupancy rates etc.)

Research into, and secondary data based on, rateable value changes, photographs, council/planning data and census data, e.g. population and employment structure, would be helpful. Additional data could come from consumer groups, university researchers, Department for Business, Enterprise and Regulatory Reform (formerly the DTI) and other interest groups.

The judgement of success requires both 'before' and 'after' commentary, or the use of a technique to show the positive and negative views of change, perhaps using an analytical technique, e.g. a bi-polar exercise.

2 **Describe and explain a programme of fieldwork and research you would use to investigate the impacts of rural rebranding strategies.**

e Answers should focus on the planning and methodology of fieldwork and the use of research sources to investigate the impacts of rebranding in a rural area.

Ideally this will involve the study of contrasting examples, such as remote rural areas versus accessible rural areas, or large-scale projects versus small-scale projects. Fieldwork, together with secondary research, should demonstrate evidence of depth of understanding across a range of areas. An alternative approach could be to examine short-term impacts against longer-term impacts of chosen strategies.

Primary sources such as oral histories and interviews, maps, visitor surveys, activity maps and questionnaires can all be used to investigate the impact of rural schemes. The schemes can vary from those that are tourist orientated, to technological improvements, to the establishment of rural enterprises and diversification schemes.

Questionnaire surveys, document analyses and environmental quality surveys are also useful techniques.

The mark scheme for these questions

Each of these Unit 2 questions will be assessed by four levels, which are written in very general terms. Essentially, therefore, the mark scheme is said to be *generic*. Below are the basic outlines of the mark scheme — it should be straightforward to see what you need to do to access each of the levels.

Level 1   (1–4 marks)
▶ Little structure.
▶ One or two basic ideas about fieldwork or research.
▶ Geographical terminology is rarely used.
▶ There are frequent written language errors.

Level 2   (5–8 marks)
▶ Some structure.
▶ Describes some fieldwork and identifies some research sources.
▶ Refers to some results.
▶ Some geographical terminology is used.
▶ There are some written language errors.

Level 3   (9–12 marks)
▶ Structured explanation of fieldwork plans, methodology and use of research sources.
▶ Uses some results effectively.
▶ Uses appropriate geographical terms and gives examples/details.
▶ Written language errors are minor.

Level 4   (13–15 marks)
▶ Structured detailed account which refers to details of student's own fieldwork and use of research sources.
▶ Explores relationships.
▶ Uses appropriate geographical terms and exemplification to show understanding. Written language errors are rare.

Unit 4 Geographical research

This unit offers six research options:
▶ Tectonic activity and hazards
▶ Cold environments — landscapes and change
▶ Life on the margins — the food supply problem
▶ The world of cultural diversity
▶ Pollution and human health at risk
▶ Consuming the rural landscape — leisure and tourism

You must select and study *one* of the options above. You should then embark on in-depth, independent and personal research on this topic. Fieldwork is an important component of this research. There is also scope for virtual fieldwork and use of GIS. You are expected to access a range of geographical information in a variety of forms: books, journals, video and the internet. You are also expected to link content and concepts from Units 1, 2 and 3 into your research.

The examination is $1\frac{1}{2}$ hours and includes pre-released material on the research focus for each option. This is released 4 weeks before the examination via the Edexcel website (**www.edexcel.org.uk**). You will be given a list of questions based on the six options and you should answer the question that relates to your chosen option. You are required to write a long essay, in which you demonstrate and synthesise the results of your research. Each question carries 70 marks. You are not allowed to take any pre-release or research materials into the exam.

The content of each option in the specification starts with the **global synoptic context**, which sets it in a wider framework to encourage synoptic links both within this unit and with Unit 3. Four topics defined by **enquiry questions** follow. Each of these must be studied because the final essay in the examination will cover two of these questions at any one time. It is recommended that you study the enquiry questions in the order given in the specification. The pre-release statement (issued 4 weeks in advance) will give a guideline as to which two enquiry questions will be focused on in the examination. The enquiry questions are followed in the specification by **suggested fieldwork opportunities**.

Tectonic activity and hazards

Global synoptic context
▶ Places — where are the tectonically active regions in the world?
▶ People — who is affected by tectonic activity and its associated hazards?
▶ Power — who is responsible for managing the risk associated with tectonic hazards?

Enquiry questions
▶ What are tectonic hazards and what causes them?
▶ What impact does tectonic activity have on landscapes and why does this impact vary?
▶ What impacts do tectonic hazards have on people and how do these impacts vary?
▶ How do people cope with tectonic hazards and what are the issues for the future?

Suggested fieldwork opportunities
▶ Local — field visits to small-scale igneous structures to study the impact of faulting/rifting on landscapes.
▶ Residential and long haul — Iceland, Italy, Arran, Skye, Lake District, north Wales.

Cold environments — landscapes and change

Global synoptic context
▶ Places — where are cold environments today?
▶ People — how populated are cold environments, and by whom?
▶ Power — who is involved in managing the threats facing cold environments today?

Enquiry questions
▶ What are cold environments and where are they found?
▶ What are the climatic processes that cause cold environments and what environmental conditions result from these?

▶ How do geomorphological processes produce distinctive landscapes and landforms in cold environments?

▶ What challenges and opportunities exist in cold environments and what management issues might result from their use?

Suggested fieldwork opportunities

▶ Local — upland areas of the UK, including alpine environments.

▶ Residential and long haul — the Alps, the Pyrenees, Norway and Iceland.

Life on the margins — the food supply problem

Global synoptic context

▶ Places — where are the 'margins'?

▶ People — who suffers from food insecurity and over-nutrition?

▶ Power — which organisations and groups are involved in ensuring food security?

Enquiry questions

▶ What are the characteristics of food supply and security?

▶ What has caused global inequalities in food supply and security?

▶ What is the role of desertification in threatening life at the margins?

▶ How effective can management strategies be in sustaining life at the margins?

Suggested fieldwork opportunities

▶ Local — sources of food including local sourcing (supermarkets, farm shops, catering establishments), local farms, fair-trade surveys.

▶ Residential and long haul — Morocco (desertification), American west (dry land management).

The world of cultural diversity

Global synoptic context

▶ Places — how do cultural landscapes vary?

▶ People — how do cultures vary?

▶ Power — is there a 'global culture'?

Enquiry questions

▶ What is the nature and value of culture in terms of people and places?

▶ How and why does culture vary spatially?

▶ How is globalisation impacting on culture?

▶ How do cultural values impact on our relationship with the environment?

Suggested fieldwork opportunities

▶ Local — urban areas exploring cultural characteristics, cultural landscapes (e.g. Wales, Cornwall), world cities such as London.

▶ Residential and long haul — Catalonia, the Basque country, Brittany, even China or parts of Africa.

Pollution and human health at risk

Global synoptic context
▶ Places — where are the polluted and unhealthy places?
▶ People — who suffers as a result of pollution and health risk?
▶ Power — who is responsible for managing these risks?

Enquiry questions
▶ What are the health risks?
▶ What are the causes of health risks?
▶ What is the link between health risk and pollution?
▶ How can the impacts of health risk be managed?

Suggested fieldwork opportunities
▶ Local — use of GIS and primary sources at a local scale, surveys of diseases and problems, surveys of types of pollution.
▶ Residential and long haul — developing-world fieldwork including surveys in Morocco and Kenya, fieldwork into pollution in distant locations, e.g. Poland (acid rain).

Consuming the rural landscape — leisure and tourism

Global synoptic context
▶ Places — where are rural areas and what are they like?
▶ People — who lives in, and visits, rural areas?
▶ Power — who manages the threats facing rural areas?

Enquiry questions
▶ What is the relationship between the growth of leisure and tourism and rural landscape use?
▶ What is the significance of some rural landscapes used for leisure and tourism?
▶ What impact does leisure and tourism have on rural landscapes?
▶ How can rural landscapes used for leisure and tourism be managed?

Suggested fieldwork opportunities
▶ Local — in-depth field study of tourism types and their impact, conflicts in a national park, research into the fragility of a rural landscape and the threats facing it.
▶ Residential and long haul — the Alps, coastal France and Spain, national parks in the USA.

Example research questions, each carrying 70 marks

Tectonic activity and hazards

1   Discuss the relationship between the nature of tectonic hazards and human responses to them.

2   Assess the relative impacts of tectonic activity on people and landscapes.

Cold environments — landscapes and change

1   To what extent can Britain's physical geography during the Quaternary be determined through the study of relict glacial and periglacial landforms?

2   Assess the extent to which the effectiveness of management strategies of cold environments depends on their location.

Life on the margins — the food supply problem

1   To what extent do food security issues vary spatially and temporally?

2   Evaluate the effectiveness of management strategies in areas facing desertification.

The world of cultural diversity

1   Discuss the ways in which cultural values affect how societies use the environment.

2   How does globalisation impact on cultural diversity in different areas of the world?

Pollution and human health at risk

1   Explain why international initiatives are increasingly needed to cope with the risks of disease and pollution.

2   Discuss the variety of health risks that exist in the world today, and their causes.

Consuming the rural landscape — leisure and tourism

1   How can models contribute to the effective management of rural landscapes experiencing demands from leisure and tourism?

2   Assess the degree to which certain rural landscapes are more suitable than others for leisure and tourism.

The mark scheme for these questions

As with Unit 2, these questions will be marked using a generic mark scheme, as given below. The mark scheme is coded and broken down into sections, each with four levels and each carrying defined amounts of marks as identified below. As with Unit 2, it should be straightforward to see what you need to do to access each of the levels.

Code D Introducing, defining and focusing on the question (10 marks)

This must include definitions of terms and a justification of the focus of the case-study selection, concepts selected and research undertaken.

0 marks — no attempt to introduce the report.

Level 1 (1–2 marks)

Limited introduction; vague definition of key terms and/or framework.

Level 2 (3–5 marks)

Some reference to title; some definitions of key terms and/or some framework.

Level 3 (6–8 marks)

Some framework/focus, by concepts and/or case studies; incomplete definitions of key terms.

Level 4 (9–10 marks)

Clear reference to title — develops a focus. Indication of framework, by concepts and/or case studies; accurate definitions of key terms.

Code R Researching and methodology (15 marks)

This must include a balanced range of case studies, with a variety of locations and possibly over time, showing evidence of detailed knowledge of them.

0 marks — case studies/concepts missing; no evidence of research.

Level 1 (1–4 marks)

Basic research; limited case-study material/concepts or lacks relevance or selection.

Level 2 (5–7 marks)

Range of case studies/concepts but lacks selection; lacks methodology/sourcing.

Level 3 (8–11 marks)

Some range (scale/location) of all/mostly relevant case studies used; some indication of methodology.

Level 4 (12–15 marks)

Wide range of relevant case studies used (scale or location); relevant concepts and/or theories used; factual topical evidence; an indication of methodology, i.e. how evidence was sampled/selected.

Code A Analysis, application and understanding (20 marks)

This section assesses your understanding and application of key ideas.

0 marks — a descriptive report lacking in detail, lacks application to question.

Level 1 (1–8 marks)

Descriptive; very limited appreciation of values/perspectives; maps/diagrams are rarely used to support answer.

Level 2 (9–12 marks)

Simple explanations; generalised material; limited appreciation of values/perspectives; maps/diagrams are sometimes used to support answer.

Level 3 (13–16 marks)

Most of the research is used to support the question; some conceptual understanding; some appreciation of values/perspectives; maps/diagrams are usually used to support answer.

Level 4 (17–20 marks)

All research applied directly to question set; high conceptual understanding; cogent argument; appreciation of different values/perspectives about the question; maps/diagrams are used to support answer.

Code C Conclusions and evaluations (15 marks)

This should involve a meaningful assessment and evaluation of the title, which may involve a return to the main case studies developed in the report.

0 marks — no conclusion or evaluation within the report.

Level 1 (1–4 marks)

An attempt at an evaluation of the question even if no end conclusion.

Level 2 (5–7 marks)

Vague conclusion, related tenuously to the question; very limited evaluations.

Level 3 (8–11 marks)

Meaningful, based on content of report; selective recall of content of report; some evaluation, either ongoing or in final conclusion.

Level 4 (12–15 marks)

Clearly stated, thorough recall of content/case studies used in essay; ongoing evaluation throughout the report; understands the complexity of the question.

Code Q Quality of written communication and sourcing (10 marks)

This is a generic mark scheme for report style writing.

0 marks — basic standards of quality of written communication not met.

Level 1 (1–2 marks)

Very basic quality of written communication; frequent spelling and punctuation errors; low level syntax; occasional use of geographical vocabulary; referenced/acknowledged material lacks evidencing/sourcing from a wide range of sources (texts, journals, internet, DVDs etc.)

Level 2 (3–5 marks)

Basic syntax, some errors of punctuation and spelling; disjointed organisation and sequencing although may have some sub-sections; some errors in punctuation and spelling; some use of appropriate geographical vocabulary; may have diagrammatic/cartographic use but rarely incorporated into text or rarely supports the argument; referenced/acknowledged material has rare evidencing/sourcing from a wide range of sources (as above).

Level 3 (6–8 marks)

Generally written with some report style sub-sections; some organisation and sequencing; good standard of punctuation and spelling; some good use of appropriate geographical vocabulary; text may have diagrammatic/cartographic use but not always incorporated into the text or supports the argument; referenced/acknowledged material: occasional evidencing/sourcing from a wide range of sources (as above).

Level 4 (9–10 marks)

Coherent structure and sequencing with obvious report style sub-sections; excellent standards of punctuation and spelling; geographical vocabulary used correctly; diagrams/maps if used incorporated into text and support argument; referenced/acknowledged material: obvious evidencing/sourcing from a wide range of sources (as above).

The OCR specification

Development of skills at AS

Students are required to develop fieldwork skills in the context of human and physical geography which relate directly to their course of study. The range of research and investigative skills should include:

▶ the use of modern technologies such as electronic image and map interpretation
▶ statistical analysis
▶ presentation techniques

Development of skills at A2

Studies at A2 should enable students to extend their research/investigative work. Both A2 units (F763 and F764) provide an opportunity for them to acquire new skills, such as more advanced statistical and analytical strategies, as well as consolidating and extending those from AS. Both units assess geographical skills, including the ability to describe and interpret features, trends and patterns from a variety of geographical sources. These should include:

▶ OS and thematic maps
▶ maps presenting statistical data
▶ data tables
▶ photographs, and satellite and other images (including GIS)
▶ various types of graph (pie, bar, line, scatter)
▶ histograms
▶ various forms of diagram including flow charts, sketch diagrams and maps
▶ the results of statistical analysis such as Spearman rank and the Mann–Whitney U test

Synoptic assessment

Synoptic assessment has been a part of all A-level geography courses for a number of years. It involves assessment of a candidate's ability to draw on his/her understanding of the connections between different aspects of the subject represented in the specification. In this context, therefore, candidates are expected to 'think like a geographer'.

Synoptic assessment is included in both A2 units and could involve the use of research and investigative skills in Unit F764 based on exemplar material drawn from work carried out at AS and in A2 Unit F763.

Unit F763 Global issues

In terms of skills, the aim of this unit is for students to develop:

▶ a knowledge of the use of modern technologies, such as GIS and remote sensing, to understand the nature and impact of global issues
▶ a knowledge and an understanding of the potential of ICT and its relevance to global issues
▶ the ability to select and use appropriate GIS skills and techniques to explore global issues
▶ the ability to carry out individual research/investigative work, including fieldwork
▶ the skills to identify, analyse and evaluate the connections between the different aspects of geography
▶ the ability to analyse and synthesise geographical information in a variety of forms and from a range of sources

▶ the ability to critically reflect on, and evaluate the potential and limitations of, approaches and methods used both inside and outside the classroom.

Unit F764 Geographical skills

The aim of this unit is for students to develop:
▶ a knowledge and an understanding of the process of geographical research, including fieldwork
▶ the skills necessary to complete a piece of individual geographical research
▶ the use of technology (e.g. remote sensing, GIS) as a research tool
▶ a knowledge and understanding of the potential of ICT and its relevance to geographical change
▶ the ability to select and use appropriate GIS skills and techniques in order to explore geographical issues including decision-making and problem-solving
▶ an awareness of the problems involved in undertaking individual geographical investigation/research
▶ an understanding that interpretation and evaluation of research results should reflect the links and connections between diverse elements of geography

It is expected that students will use skills in geographical research and investigations/fieldwork that they have acquired during their AS and A2 courses. As part of their course, students will need to have undertaken individual research on a geographical topic of their choice. This individual research/investigation should be based on any topic that is covered within units F761 and F762 (the AS units), and F763 (A2 unit), and should provide clear evidence of extension and synthesis of understanding and skills.

A student's investigations should follow the stages listed below.

Stage 1 Identify a suitable geographical question or hypothesis for investigation
The question/hypothesis should be:
▶ at a suitable scale
▶ capable of research
▶ clearly defined and of a clear geographical nature
▶ based upon wider geographical theories, ideas, concepts or processes

Stage 2 Develop a plan and strategy for conducting the investigation
When developing a plan and strategy, the student is required to:
▶ identify the data needed to examine the question/hypothesis posed
▶ establish appropriate strategies and methods for collecting the necessary data — this should include sampling where appropriate
▶ gain an understanding of the limitations imposed by the resources and the time available for the investigation

▶ appreciate the potential risks in undertaking the research and to understand methods of minimising any risk

Stage 3 Collect and record data appropriate to the geographical question/hypothesis

When collecting and recording data, students are required to:

▶ use primary and secondary data as appropriate to the question/hypothesis posed (you should consult the earlier sections of this book titled 'Collecting primary data' and 'Collecting secondary data' in order to establish what is meant by each of these categories)

▶ describe and explain the different ways of collecting/recording data

▶ be aware of the need for accuracy and reliability before, during and after the process of data collection

Stage 4 Present the data collected in appropriate forms

When presenting the data that have been collected/recorded, students are required to:

▶ use appropriate techniques to present the data, including maps, diagrams, graphs and annotated photographs (you should consult the earlier section in this book titled 'Presenting your results')

▶ make sure that presented material is organised in a logical way in relation to the analysis

▶ maintain a high standard of presentation of the material relevant to the question/hypothesis posed

Stage 5 Analysing and interpreting the data

This stage requires students to:

▶ describe the findings shown by the data presentation

▶ where appropriate, analyse the data further, using statistical techniques (you should consult the earlier section of this book titled 'The analysis and interpretation of data')

▶ interpret the results in relation to the original question/hypothesis posed

▶ explain patterns found and any anomalous results

Stage 6 Present a summary of the findings and an evaluation of the investigation

Students are required to:

▶ use evidence presented in the previous stage to provide a clear conclusion to the investigation, which relates back specifically to the original question/hypothesis posed

▶ attempt an evaluation of the extent to which the study supports, or otherwise, the general geographical theories, ideas and concepts being studied

▶ make an evaluation of the limitations of the study in terms of the methods used and the data collected, and make suggestions for possible improvements

Assessment

You will be assessed through paper F764, which is titled 'Geographical skills' and represents 20% of the total A-level (AS and A2 combined) marks. The paper lasts $1\frac{1}{2}$ hours.

There are two sections, each with different types of question.

Section A

In this section candidates will be set three questions, of which they are required to answer one. These questions will be based upon stimulus material such as maps, photographs, satellite images, graphs, diagrams, cross sections, statistical and written material, and will require candidates to use the skills and techniques acquired during the geographical research undertaken at both AS and A2.

Section B

In this section two questions will be set and candidates are expected to answer both of them. They will be based on the investigation carried out as part of Unit F764 and candidates must state the title of their investigation before they start to answer. Questions will focus on the skills and techniques used during that geographical research, including analysis, interpretation, evaluation and drawing conclusions.

Example questions

Below you will find three questions. Questions 1 and 2 are typical of those set in Section A, one based upon a physical geography topic and the second on a human topic. Question 3 reflects those set in Section B. Following each question there is a mark scheme that will give you an insight into the kind of answer expected by the examiners.

Example question 1

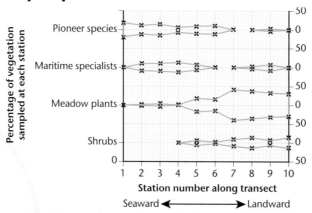

Figure 1 Kite diagram showing the results of vegetation quadrat sampling across a sand dune system in south Devon

Site	1	2	3	4	5	6	7	8	9	10
Distance inland (m)	5.0	11.5	15.0	21.5	29.0	34.5	38.0	45.0	50.5	58.0
Soil depth (cm)	0.1	1.0	1.8	2.4	2.4	10.7	12.2	11.8	6.7	15.4
Soil pH	7.8	7.2	7.0	6.9	6.5	6.0	6.2	4.5	5.8	5.3
Plant height (m)	2.4	2.3	4.2	4.0	6.8	11.4	10.0	14.7	23.8	52.5

Table 1 Variations across the sand dune system which was the location for the quadrat sampling shown in Figure 1

Figure 1 and Table 1 represent some of the results of a geographical investigation carried out in south Devon. The aim of the investigation was to examine how the vegetation changed across a sand dune area and to provide possible explanations for the changes noted.

The research question was 'How and why does vegetation change across the sand dune area of this part of south Devon?'

a Evaluate the effectiveness of Figure 1 and Table 1 in representing the data used to answer the above research question.   (5 marks)

b How can statistical and computer-based techniques be used in the analysis of variables that contribute to vegetation change in a succession?   (10 marks)

c Suggest, with reference to other geographical factors, why the results from such an investigation of variations in vegetation types might be unreliable.   (5 marks)

(Total: 20 marks)

Mark scheme

Section a

🖉 The kite diagram shows types of vegetation with distance, therefore it does show change across an area. It also shows the amount of each vegetation type at each recording station, giving a straightforward comparison. This is visually effective but as it only looks at species of vegetation there is no information given on other features such as vegetation height, amount of ground cover etc. It would be possible to add other measures to the kite diagram, such as acidity (pH), wind speed and aspect. This would enable you to begin to link the vegetation changes to possible causal factors.

Level 1   A limited evaluation is given of Figure 1 and Table 1 with an unbalanced range of advantages and limitations. Very little, if any, linkage to the actual question or the figures given.   (0–3 marks)

Level 2   A clear evaluation of Figure 1 and Table 1 giving a wide range of advantages and limitations well linked to the question. Clear references made to the figures.   (4–5 marks)

Section b

e Statistical techniques could include correlation techniques of different kinds (e.g. Spearman rank correlation coefficient) and descriptive statistics such as mean, median etc.

Computer-based techniques could include satellite images or remote sensing of variables such as soil moisture content, acidity (pH), salinity and organic matter content, as well as programs that run correlation techniques.

Examples could be drawn from the candidate's own fieldwork to show how such techniques could be used to measure the variables.

Level 1   A technique may be described which is not wholly appropriate to demonstrating the relationship between distance and vegetation on such a section across a sand dune area. Candidates are also unable to provide an explanation of why the chosen technique may be effective in analysing the variables. More than one technique may be identified but the candidate is unable to say how these are relevant to making the correlation between vegetation and distance.   (0–4 marks)

Level 2   A limited (at least two) range of appropriate techniques for making the correlation between distance and vegetation is put forward. There is also an explanation as to why these techniques are effective in the analysis of such variables. It is possible to describe techniques which are only partly appropriate, but if the candidate is able to provide a reasonable explanation of why such a technique may be effective in this type of analysis, then the answer can be assessed within this level.   (5–7 marks)

Level 3   The candidate clearly describes a range of appropriate techniques that can be used and explains in detail why the chosen techniques are effective in analysing the variables that contribute to vegetation change along such a section of sand dunes.   (8–10 marks)

Section c

e Answers here could cover a wide range of factors:
▶ Human factors could include fires, planting vegetation, amounts of trampling.
▶ Environmental factors could include microclimates, rainfall amounts and intensity, wildlife, wind action.
▶ Any of these could play a role that complicates the simple succession of vegetation.
▶ Factors that impact upon the carrying out of the investigation are relevant to this question.

Level 1   Only limited suggestions are made (superficial range or only one factor investigated) with reference to appropriate factors, with little, if any, reference to the reliability of the investigation.   (0–3 marks)

Level 2   Detailed suggestions (two or more) of appropriate factors with clear cause–effect established on the reliability of the investigation. Synopticity is demonstrated within the answer.   (4–5 marks)

Example question 2

Figures 2 and 3 show the area in and around London, and this material is being used as part of a survey that has the aim of studying land-use patterns in the capital.

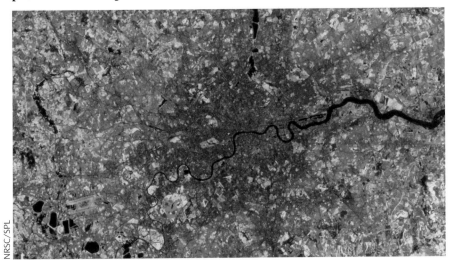

Figure 2 False colour satellite image of London. (In the examination a colour photograph would be produced for this question)

NRSC/SPL

One of the research questions in this survey is 'How does the land use vary, in both type and intensity, with distance from the centre of the city?'

a   With reference to Figures 2 and 3, assess the suitability of this method for gathering such information.   (5 marks)

b   How can statistical and computer-based techniques be used in the analysis of patterns of land use?   (10 marks)

c   Outline the uses of GIS in geographical modelling and simulations.
                    (5 marks)
                    (Total: 20 marks)

Mark scheme

Section a

☑ Satellite photographs are useful in that they give the land-use data at the time that they were taken (a 'snapshot'). This enables the land use at that particular time to be studied but it also allows comparisons to be made through time as many images can be viewed. Other factors than distance from the city centre could influence land-use intensity, but no other information is given.

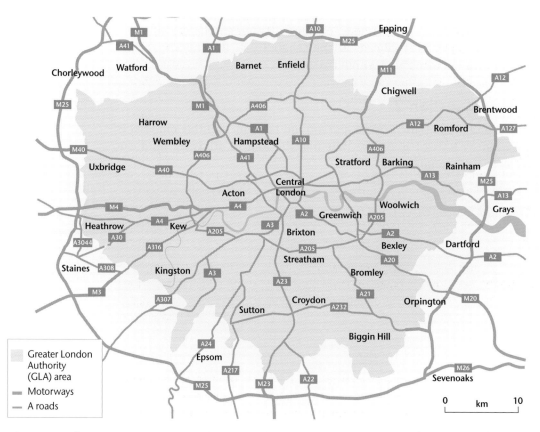

Figure 3 Road map of London and its environs

Level 1 An assessment is made in a very limited way as to the suitability of a satellite image in researching the question with a limited appreciation of its strengths and weaknesses. The answer is not balanced with far more of one aspect. Very little reference is made to Figures 2 and 3 in support of the answer. (0–3 marks)

Level 2 Clear assessment made of the suitability of a satellite image in researching this question with a clear appreciation of its strengths and weaknesses. The answer is supported by reference to the image. (4–5 marks)

Section b

e Statistical techniques could include a number of correlation methods such as the chi-squared test, Spearman rank and nearest neighbour analysis, or descriptive statistics such as mean and median.

Computer-based techniques could include other satellite images or remote sensing of variables such as drainage density, gradient and vegetation, as well as computer-based correlation techniques.

Level 1   Answers may describe a technique that is not wholly appropriate for the analysis of patterns of land use and may not put forward an explanation as to why the chosen technique may be effective in this case. More than one technique may be simply identified but the candidate makes no real attempt to show how these techniques can be used in this particular investigation.   (0–4 marks)

Level 2   A limited (at least two) range of techniques is presented which could make the correlation between distance and land use. There is also an explanation as to why these techniques are effective in the analysis of such variables. It is possible to describe techniques which are only partly appropriate, but if the candidate is able to provide a reasonable explanation as to why such techniques may be effective in this type of analysis, then answers can be assessed within this level.   (5–7 marks)

Level 3   Candidates clearly describe a range of appropriate techniques that can be used for this purpose. They then go on to explain in detail why the chosen techniques are effective in analysing patterns of land use.   (8–10 marks)

Section c

🖉 In one sense GIS is an information system capable of integrating, storing, editing, analysing and displaying geographical information. It is also a tool allowing users to analyse spatial information, edit data and maps, and present the results of these operations.

Answers will generally reflect the experience of the candidate in geographical modelling and simulation. GIS enables researchers to simplify reality, allowing the interaction of a range of variables in order to identify patterns and trends.

Level 1   The answer outlines a very limited range of the uses of GIS, in either a limited range of geographical modelling/simulations or with a focus on either models or simulations. Little reference is made to specific examples.   (0–3 marks)

Level 2   Answer outlines a range of uses for GIS in a range of geographical modelling and simulations. All is well supported by reference to specific examples.   (4–5 marks)

Example question 3

Write the title of your geographical investigation.

State the nature of the fieldwork investigation that you conducted during your A-level course. What was the conclusion(s) to your investigation? How did you reach it/them and to what extent was it/were they geographically sound and relevant? (20 marks)

Mark scheme

There are four elements to this question:

1 Candidates are required to make introductory statements with regard to the nature of their investigation.

2 Clear reference must be made to the conclusions. This must be very specific and relate to the hypothesis or research question that is being investigated.

3 The description of how the conclusions were reached should focus on the interpretation of the analysis rather than simple methodology.

4 The evaluation must relate strongly to some geographical concept or model. There will be clear discrimination here between the best answers and those that merely state that the conclusions did match the theory involved in the investigation.

Level 1

1 Simple statement of the nature of the investigation, probably nothing more than a repeat of the title which they have already given.

2/3 Very limited explanations offered of the conclusions reached and very vague about how they were obtained.

4 Little, if any, evaluation of the extent to which the conclusions are related to a particular geographical model or concept or related to the question or hypothesis stated. Candidates offer a very limited explanation of the methods used. (0–9 marks)

Level 2

1 Some detail on the nature of the investigation. The information represents more than just a simple title.

2/3 Candidates explain the conclusions reached and how they were obtained.

4 An evaluation of the extent to which the conclusions are related to a particular geographical model or concept is expected along with some relation to the research question or hypothesis. (10–15 marks)

Level 3

1 A good account of the nature of the investigation.

2/3 Candidates explain in detail the conclusions reached and how they were obtained.

4 A detailed evaluation is made of the extent to which the conclusions relate to a particular geographical model or concept. This is clearly related to the question or hypothesis stated. (16–20 marks)